The Contemplative Paddler's Fireside Companion

The Contemplative Paddler's Fireside Companion

By

Timothy McDonnell

NORTH STAR PRESS OF ST. CLOUD, INC.
St. Cloud, Minnesota

ISBN: 978-1-68201-022-8

This is a work of non-fiction. Some of the names have been altered in deference to privacy.

First Edition: May 2016

Printed in the United States of America.

Published by
North Star Press
P.O. Box 451
St. Cloud, MN 56302

www.northstarpress.com

*For my paddle trip companions over the many
years and many miles,
and for my beloved Maggie.*

Table of Contents

"This is the true joy in life, the being used for a purpose recognized by yourself as a mighty one; the being thoroughly worn out before you are thrown on the scrap heap; the being a force of Nature instead of a feverish selfish little clod of ailments and grievances complaining that the world will not devote itself to making you happy."

~ George Bernard Shaw

Come Sit by the Fire

RUMINATION SEEMS EASY and natural around a good fire. It has been my experience that companions are typically more honest, more open, and more themselves around a campfire than elsewhere. I now bring to my campfire both reverence and reflection in equal measure, and it has been a long journey getting here. As is the case with many dreamers in the summer of their years, I was often rash, reckless, and in time regretful. These days find me with a perpetual snow on my head and in my beard. With so much life in the rearview and so many memories from which to choose, it is becoming easier now to balance each grimace with a chuckle. Growth and gratitude have come into greater alignment.

When I am alone with a fire, I am usually writing. I have been a lover of the written word for almost as long as I have been in love with canoe tripping. Until it became lost in one of several relocations during my college days, I had a small canvas ditty bag filled with paddle-trip keepsakes that were dear to me. Inside were a handful of agates, a couple of gold nuggets comprised mostly of iron pyrite, the broken point off a moose antler, and three colored glass beads I felt certain were of fur-trade origin. There was also a small scroll of birch-bark on which I penciled at age twelve a simple reference to the awe I felt camping beneath tall white pines. This I wrote while on my first canoe trip longer than a simple overnight. There was nothing profound here, mind you, but the words and images came from an innocent and reverent heart. To my childish self, the wind in the tall pines was actually the breath of God. Writing, then, was something akin to a form of prayer.

I became a prolific letter writer during my high school years, when it was important to me to keep in contact with canoe trip buddies during the long winter months. Keeping a journal during each paddle trip became habitual, something I practice to this day. Were I of the millennial generation rather than a child of the baby boom, you could assume with accuracy that I would ride the same swell as my peers, each of us umbilically attached to a smart phone or a smarter tablet, taking in a pixelated view of the universe. Digitized communication, though, seems to be all about expediency. I have tried over the decades to be all about clarity.

The many old journal books I keep on the shelves in my den serve as memory pieces. They rekindle and take me to places of joy, energy, experience, and transformation. I am now my own ditty bag. My heart and mind are filled with paddle trip memories both trying and tremendous.

Before using a good campfire as a setting for contemplation, I like to put it to work. Reflection is central to my preferred method of campfire cooking. When time and weather permit, nothing enhances a trail meal quite like a coffeecake, a bannock, or a pan of gingerbread fresh from the reflector oven. Fully collapsible and comprised of sheeted tin or aluminum hinged or slotted together to form a triangular box with a center shelf, this apparatus is simplicity itself. Set next to an open fire to catch and reflect heat, the oven bakes anything placed upon its shelf quickly and efficiently, so long as the user is attentive. Consider the natural attraction of an evening fire, and then couple this with the tantalizing aromas of warm baked goods. People are going to gather. If you are a dozy soul susceptible to letting yourself get pulled into a fireside gabfest and away from the task at hand, this device is not for you. Scorch a pan of brownies just once, and you are likely to be relegated to dish detail for the remainder of your paddle trip. Do the job well, and you become the James Beard of the backwoods. Most paddlers tend to fixate on food. It is not just an army that travels on its stomach.

A good fire can be a lifesaver. I can recall a few occasions where signs of hypothermia in a trip member ignited a frenetic scramble to get to shore and get a mighty warm-up blaze going. On my first canoe trip to Hudson Bay in the summer of 1977, it rained twenty-eight out of our thirty days. Wind and wet steadily sapped us of whatever heat we generated from calories and constant paddling. Building a fire to thaw extremities became routine, and we began packing a stash of dry kindling for emergencies. The high school boys my friend John Edmundson and I led on this trip got in the habit of rolling large stones into each mid-day fire. When it came time to return to the water, they carefully rolled the hot stones out and used them as foot warmers in the cold aluminum canoes for as long as the heat remained. An excerpt from my journal for this first of several Seal River canoe trips illustrates our hot lunch ritual, and the establishment of rituals became one of the running jokes of this trip.

Picture yourself in the Land of Little Sticks. It is not quite tundra, but the trees in this section of northern Manitoba are noticeably puny and scarce. There is not much in this part of the Hudson Bay watershed to block the wind.

Coming to shore for lunch is a task not to be taken lightly here. The river current must be reckoned with carefully. The same is true for the shoreline itself. Both banks are stony. Beyond the boulders of each shoreline is an expanse of dense willow thicket stretching thirty yards or more to stands of stunted spruce.

Our group of eleven works to secure the canoes, and we take from the packs the food items, utensils, and wood tools we need for a warm-up fire and a hot lunch of soup. Trudging through the thicket, we clear a spot for lunch in the shelter of the spruce trees. Old tree roots and mountains of tinder twigs are gathered, and we quickly get a fire going. The soup feels good going down. It warms the belly, and the fire brings cheer to the grayness.

Next comes the balancing ritual. This starts with a green willow stick pointed at one end. You firmly spear your ration of cervelat sausage horizontally and some-

4

times duck to avoid getting a jab in the ear from the sticks of your neighbors. You turn to the fire with your savored jewel. A few attentive minutes get the sizzle juices flowing. Next it is on to the critical second stage. Having scored your daily portion of Colby cheese, you gingerly set this atop your partly seared sausage. Then you must once again shoulder your way in and secure your spot at the rim of the fire to roast both cheese and meat together. You must take great care, as ten other bodies are crowded around the fire, each aware of nothing in the world save his own stick, his own cheese, and his own cervelat. If through some gracious gift of fate another's elbow or a shift in the burning wood does not topple the whole works into the ash heap, your day is made and so is your lunch. Woe to you if your stars are misaligned and your sizzling treasure takes an irretrievable tumble into the heap. Nothing is quite so bleak on such a day as a newly doused fire pit full of soggy, lifeless ash. There, amid the dismal gray mess, are the shriveled remains of what might have brought you joy as well as sustenance.

Perhaps the simplest pleasures truly are the most valuable. The adversity these details bring to mind may spell total misery. On the contrary, this was one of my all-time favorite paddle trips, and I am not alone in that sentiment. Life was simplified on this trip, and all that was required for contentment was to be warm, to be dry, and to have your belly full.

When I was a small boy, I used to watch the canoe groups heading across Hungry Jack Lake. My parents owned a resort on the lake, located thirty-two miles into the boreal forest from the village of Grand Marais, Minnesota. Most of the paddlers I watched from the resort dock began their trek at the YMCA canoe camp one lake to the north. The camp specialized in introducing people to the Boundary Waters Canoe Area Wilderness and to Ontario's adjacent Quetico Provincial Park. Westbound groups always seemed to zigzag down the lake, noisily hitting the canoe gunwales with their paddles. Canoes in the same group were often widely scattered. There was typically shouting and sometimes loud cursing as paddlers new to the sport and as green as the trees tried to adjust to their surroundings.

Eastbound canoe groups were much different and a true joy to watch. The canoes of such a group typically moved over the water efficiently on a straight course, with suntanned paddlers working in unison, heading home from their shared wilderness journey. In place of gunwale-banging clatter, songs often rose from these groups. As I watched from the dock, I experienced a rhythm that I could see in the fluid paddle strokes. It thrilled me each time a paddler returned my wave, and I would keep waving until the last canoe passed around the point and out of sight. Something magical happened to people out there on a paddle trip. The good woods had a wonderful way of changing people for the better. I did not fully comprehend what exactly happened out there, but I sure wanted a part of it.

In time, I became a canoe camper, exploring the millions of acres of wilderness that constituted my backyard. I experienced the transformational power of a paddle trip firsthand, and I often witnessed its life-changing effects in those with whom I journeyed. What happened out there had much to do with a restorative process of simplification. Stripping life down to what you can fit in your packsack and what you are willing to haul across a portage is a wonderfully cathartic exercise. Forcing yourself to become nomadic permits a greater connection with your surroundings. When it is done properly, this is an extremely peace-giving and life-affirming set of experiences.

There was a fire ritual at the canoe camp I attended when I was a boy. Campers who had distinguished themselves during each canoe trip were presented with both an honor and a challenge the night before returning home. After a sauna and a huge chicken dinner at the canoe base, there was always a campfire. As the evening wound down, the canoe trip guides chose one or two campers, pulling them away from the group and away from a good night of sleep. Those selected were given a challenge. Could they stay awake all night and tend a fire alone in the wilderness?

Each person accepting the challenge to become a keeper of the fire was put into a canoe and taken to a solitary spot across the lake from the camp. Before being left alone for the night, the honoree was given a water bucket, a leather pouch, and one torch. The torch would only last for about one hour, so it had to be used to start a fire that would still be blazing at sunrise. Within the circle of firelight, the honoree collected sticks and brushwood for fuel. The water bucket was for safety, but it was also central to temptation. Why not simply cave in, douse the fire, and go to sleep on a bed of moss? Inside the leather pouch was a pencil stub and a set of index cards, and on each card was a thought-provoking question along with plenty of space to write a response. Once confident the fire was well underway, the honoree could spend a bit of time in contemplation and jot down what came to mind.

A successful keeper of the fire would have a cheerful little blaze going when the sun broke the horizon and a canoe arrived for the return trip to the base. A strong sense of satisfaction offset weariness, and there was actual joy in drowning the fire that took such effort to maintain. The fire keeper's name would be added to an honor roll, and the honoree would be acknowledged at breakfast. He or she would receive a small leather memory piece simply enscribed with a picture of a campfire and words in the language of the French-Canadian voyageurs: *Gardien du Feu*, or Keeper of the Fire.

My own night of fire keeping came at the end of the same canoe trip on which I created my birchbark scroll. I had a blaze at dawn. In the leather pouch were the index cards with my set of scribbled answers. Aided by the light of a fire, ever an adherent to ritual, I have been trying to come up with answers to thought-provoking questions ever since.

While still in high school, I became a canoe camp counselor. Instruction was a purpose I recognized as mighty. It fit the person I wished to become. My appetite for the peace of the boreal forest became a principle force in my life. Moving farther north and deeper into the good woods, I teamed up with a close friend and we began to guide canoe trips into the sub-Arctic and the Hudson Bay watershed. I was raised to always share a good thing, and I found plentiful blessings in helping other trekkers make their own wilderness discoveries. Keeping a journal on each paddle trip helped to keep the best of my own discoveries fresh and alive. This made the sharing easier. I discovered long ago that the stillness of the water at a windless dawn leads one to acknowledge the existence of a force far greater than any of us. Whatever this force may be, it is something meant to be shared. It is as present in the perfection of a still morning as it is in the roar of a mighty waterfall.

Eventually, I turned my attention to Lake Superior. In my continual attempts to peel back life to its bare essentials, I transitioned from the relative luxury of a voluminous tripping canoe to the limited capacity of a snug sea kayak. In doing so, I discovered anew how little I require to be truly content. An open heart, an open mind, and a reverent spirit take up little space, and they make all the difference in a successful journey. When I discovered kayaking, I gave up guiding and became a client, taking great pleasure in learning from adventurous people half my age while paddling the largest freshwater lake on the planet.

The solitude I derive from time spent in the wilderness has more to do with the presence of symmetry than with the absence of sound. When the world is too much with me, I begin to hunger for simplification and sensory balance. My body has never learned to calmly adjust to a surfeit of extraneous noise. I was born with a significant sensorineural hearing loss affecting both ears. Compounding that is a condition I experience known as auditory recruitment. To help deal with the deficit caused by malfunctioning nerve endings in the inner ear, the brain of a person with this condition tries to compensate by redirecting or recruiting healthy nerve endings to fill in the gaps. This can and often does result in a distortion of the signals reaching the brain. They are perceived as being much louder than they were ever intended. Fortunately, I grew up in an environment where both peace and quiet were readily attainable.

My loved ones can certainly attest that I am a different type of animal when too long shorebound. The sense of calm so easily obtained when on the water rapidly evaporates as I become absorbed by the demands of my shorebound life. My nervous system responds to the dissonance by taking on the semblance of an overwound clock spring. Acid drips into my belly and too often shows up in my words. As my spirit sags and my soul begins to stagnate, I become hard company for others. Balance comes from planning my next paddle trip, from poring over maps, from touching my kayak or canoe and having them near. Solace comes from sitting by the fireplace at home rereading the paddle trip journals I have written over the past four decades. It comes from having the faith to dream again and from believing I will soon be out amid the waves once more.

I have learned what to bring along for my journey and what to discard. Pencils and a journal are always part of my kit. They permit a means of sharing a good thing. If that sharing takes place around a fire, we are doubly blessed. It is through the acts of sharing and reflection that this pilgrim is learning to keep peace alive when he is yet caught up in his shorebound self. I have been abundantly blessed finding a pathway to joy and fulfillment early in my life. The choices I have been fortunate to make for myself have sharpened my focus. They continue to keep me well-connected to the wild. Since I am fully aware of the value of my circumstances, I am fully cognizant of my obligation to share the blessings. There is room enough here. Come sit by the fire.

A Grand Near Miss

WHEN AN ENTIRE bush community has been praying for rain for ten weeks and eleven transients petition the Lord for sunshine, who is going to be the winner? The Ministry of Natural Resources had issued a fire ban covering the town of Leaf Rapids, Manitoba, and its surrounding forest. When our motley band of paddlers rolled into the area in an absurdly overloaded Volkswagen Microbus, the weather began to sour dramatically. Had we more of an entrepreneurial bend, each of us could have made a killing hiring out as itinerant rainmakers.

In the summer of 1976, my friend John Edmundson decided to break with the canoe camp we both worked for and start up his own venture. Recruiting teenaged clients from the private academy where he was employed as a math teacher, John began offering extended paddle trips in Manitoba and northwestern Ontario. He named his venture *Pays-d'en-Haut*, which is French for "the upper country." It refers to Canada's interior, the land the voyageurs wintered in bartering for fur. It is a region within the great boreal forest that stretches east to west from Hudson Bay to beyond the Alberta foothills, and south to north from Lake of the

Woods to the sub-Arctic barrens. That is a mighty large chunk of geography. There you will find plenty of scope for an adventurous imagination and enough wilderness water to sustain a wandering soul for several lifetimes. As John and I both had a passion for whitewater canoeing and a desire to explore ever farther into the Canadian bush, I joined him as a co-guide during his second summer season. We put together a thirty-day canoe trip set to go from Leaf Rapids, Manitoba, to the town of Churchill on Hudson Bay.

Our route was both brutal and spectacular. Beginning on Southern Indian Lake, we worked our way up a series of small lakes and connecting creeks into the headwaters of the South Seal River. This river took us to Shethanei Lake, a gatherer of waters. Both the South Seal River and the North Seal River empty into Shethanei. The outflow at the northeastern end of this lake is the Seal River proper, and this forms one mighty ride all the way to tidewater.

Theoretically, our crew of eleven followed an old winter portage route once we left Southern Indian Lake. Area Cree living on the lake seemed to feel we actually could connect the dots and make our way to Big Sand Lake and the South Seal River headwaters, albeit not without some serious effort. A winter portage route typically skirts swampy areas and rapids that are hazardous to a dog sled or a snowmobile. It usually favors the higher ground, and that can run a long way from the water. A group of paddlers, by contrast, favors a watercourse. Once our crew was well along this route and fully committed to it, we found ourselves eating up a great deal of time bushwhacking trails from one small lake to another.

Adversity can destroy a team effort and shatter the attainment of a shared goal. On the other hand, adversity can pull a crew together and bring out the best qualities of each member. The crew John and I led was phenomenal. Never in all my years of doing paddle trips and working as a teacher have I ever met a group of young men quicker to laugh, more willing to pull together to finish a task, or more eager for adventure. Most of these fellows were raised in affluence. A few came from broken homes. No two personalities were entirely alike. The great equalizer for this group was our having to deal with the constant rain, coupled with the need to push farther each day. No one was any more or any less comfortable than his mates. No one had it any easier, and no one held the monopoly on hard work.

Paddling songs became portage-building songs. These added some degree of levity to the chore of blazing trails and hauling across all our packs and canoes. Of course, a sick mind is a terrible thing to waste. It took no time at all for the lyrics to become a bit twisted. Take as an example the French-Canadian nonsense song "*Mon Merle a Perdu Son Bec*" ("My Blackbird has Lost its Beak"), which actually was a voyageur paddling song. The song in its original form is bizarre enough, as it essentially asks: How is my blackbird going to sing after it loses in rapid succession all of its major body parts? Our version became something of a theme song as we worked together day after rainy day.

Come to the Pays-d'en-Haut
Come to the Pays-d'en-Haut
You'll expire in a mire
of inky black Jell-o.

Come to the Pays-d'en-Haut
Come to the Pays-d'en-Haut
Carve a trail watch it fail
You'll be filled with woe.

Come to the Pays-d'en-Haut
Come to the Pays-d'en-Haut
It's a pain in the rain
Wait until it snows.

None of us was particularly keen on country music, but that did not stop us from bastardizing a Tammy Wynette classic that has her spelling out all the hurting words of her d-i-v-o-r-c-e. In our less-than-capable hands, this went as follows:

Our paddle trip is nine days old and looking rather bleak.
My sleeping bag is sopping wet, and brother, does it reek!
Well, I spell out all the hurting words and turn my head
when I speak,
'cuz we won't get to Big Sand Lake for at least another week.
Our p-o-r-t-a-g-e continues today.

Me and c-a-n-o-e might be going astray.
Well, I love the woods but this will be pure H-E-double-L
on me.
Oh, I wish that we could stop this p-o-r-t-a-g-e.

In this manner we carved our passage through the Slough of Despond, pushing ever forward. This type of musical encouragement may not have made the muskeg any drier underfoot, but it did help take the edge off the snotty weather. Our final trail was a bush-whack from Hurst Lake to Big Sand Lake, comprised of a horrendous two-and-a-half-mile slog through and around a maze of spruce bogs, creek beds, and downed trees. By the time this portage was behind us, we were working well as one tight unit. Our crew had crossed into a new watershed. We were finished with bogs and small creeks. Ahead were big lakes, big rivers, and wide-open horizons.

Big lakes are liberating, and this is especially true after many days spent hacking a trail through a tunnel of trees. However, big winds can hamper that sense of freedom, and our group encountered plenty of wind. John figured we need never bother taking a compass reading, for as long as there was a headwind, we were paddling in the right direction. We often compensated by rising in the wee hours to put as many miles behind us as we could before the wind rose. When the wind and waves kept us shorebound, it was often at a spot where we could hike atop an esker to have a good look at the country. Eskers, long ridges of glacial till left over from the last ice age some ten to twelve thousand years ago, were new to most of our group. They seem to me to be the raw, exposed bones of this northern wilderness. Often you will find evidence of moose or caribou having used an esker ridge as a trail. The higher ground catches more of the breeze and gives these creatures respite from the plaguing swarms of black flies and mosquitoes. Of course, that is precisely the reason we always chose to camp atop an esker when given the option.

When it came time to run rapids, the pulse of each member of our crew would quicken dramatically. John had done his homework in preparing us for the Seal River and its whitewater. A small handful of canoe trippers had shared their river experiences with him, and John used this information to charge our enthusiasm. We had a sizeable collection of annotated maps, trip notes, and diagrams from generous folks, all of whom wished us well and emphasized our need for caution. Many of our crewmembers had accumulated some experience running swifts in the Boundary Waters Canoe Area Wilderness. A few of the fellows were familiar with larger whitewater, having paddled the previous summer with John on Manitoba's Bloodvein River. With their power, length, and sheer numbers, the rapids of the Seal River were of a magnitude far greater than any of us had ever negotiated. John and I were thankful for all of the helpful advice other travelers down this mighty river had supplied. We heeded the warnings. Drizzle-sodden, shivering, and pumped with adrenaline, we left Shethanei Lake and made our run toward Hudson Bay.

At the time of this first *Pays-d'en-Haut* Seal River trip, neither John nor I had fully mastered the art of running whitewater by going slower than the current. This method would have us applying backstrokes, pry strokes, sweeps, and cross-ferrying techniques to successfully work our way down to the tail end of each major set of rapids. As an alternative to running a set faster than the current, slowing down permits much greater control. By moving slower than the current, you have more time to decide on your course. You pivot easier, without momentum determining the course for you. Once mastered, this slowing down is much safer than barreling hell-for-leather downstream. It is also a great deal of fun.

We negotiated all the rapids of the South Seal River running faster than the current, as that was the skill set we had at the time. There was no mishap save for one swamp that had three of the fellows wet, cold, a little frightened, but basically fine. Our crew learned fast that the water was killer cold and not a place for the foolhardy. The rivers of our collected experience were all farther south, much warmer, and all a great deal more forgiving than the Seal. Dumping in a rapid previously had meant just a wild swim, embarrassment, and maybe a little razzing from your mates. Dumping on the Seal with this unseasonably cold weather might literally be the last thing you would ever do.

An underwater rock ledge extending four-fifths of the way across a wide river is not going to get out of your way. There is just such a ledge well upstream of the tail end of a magnificent stretch of Seal River white-water called Nine Bar Rapids. Canadian topographical maps use a slash mark, or bar, across the river as a symbol for a major piece of whitewater. The larger the rapids, the greater the number of slash marks. Nine Bar Rapids is certainly major, as it runs about three miles. Our crew walked the four canoes down the first one hundred yards or so before starting to shoot. Then each of us in turn piled aboard his assigned craft wild with anticipation and fully ready for a carnival ride. The ledge was not marked on our maps. It had about a four-foot drop that was totally obscured by the sur-rounding whitewater and fully undistinguishable until we were right on top of it.

My canoe was third in line. We left plenty of time and distance between each canoe to avoid running into each other. By the time I reached the ledge, the two previous canoes were out of sight downriver. When I saw the frothy mess immediately ahead of us, all of my wild anticipation evaporated in a flash. Bug-eyed terror rushed in to fill the void. Suddenly we were caught in Niagara aboard a china cup. Trying to avoid the center drop head on, my bowman and I quickly angled the canoe and skirted over the ledge. It was our last-ditch effort to try to stay upright, but it was not enough. We shipped a great deal of water, swamped, and bobbed along holding onto the canoe for the remaining mile of the rapids.

The river was shockingly cold. A thousand thoughts flashed fast and furiously through my brain as we bobbed along. My bowman and I soon realized that we were pretty much helpless until the current slowed. Each time we tried to get to shore, we hit a short rush that kept us in the center channel. Each time it seemed shallow enough for us to try to gain purchase on our footing and right the canoe, the current either swept us off our feet or caused the canoe to start to roll on top of us. All we could do was ride it out and pray no one was hurt.

The river widened and slowed a bit, but we still could not get to shore. Then we saw John, his bowman, and his canoe up on the left bank. They were all right, but they yelled to us that they had no paddles. That meant they were in no position to come to our aid. John tried to tell us that the second canoe had made it through successfully and that its trio of paddlers was up ahead with a fire going. It was not until we saw the trio that we understood what John was trying to convey. These three kept their wits about them and expertly did what they needed to do. One member of the trio was busy tending the fire and working to warm the third fellow from John's canoe, who had gotten separated from his mates. The other two quickly helped haul my bowman, my canoe, and me out of the river. Though the fire looked wonderfully inviting, I was busy trying to do a head count. There was as yet no sign of the fourth canoe and no sign of any of its three crewmembers.

All of my packs were still strapped into my canoe when we pulled it ashore. I was still holding onto my paddle. My heart sank when I looked upriver and saw one pack and the fourth canoe come bobbing down on the current. Where were its three paddlers? John and I were strict about making certain no one even touched a canoe in any rapids without first putting on a life jacket. One positive consequence of the persistent rain and chilly weather was our habitually wearing life jackets as much for their added warmth as for their floatation. John and I had also emphasized the standard safety practice of staying with the canoe in the event of a capsize. Even a swamped canoe will not sink. None of this was looking good.

After we had retrieved the lone pack and the fourth canoe, I sent a canoe across the river with an extra paddle to give to John. Minutes later, the rest of us spied our missing threesome walking along the left bank toward John. They had two of their packs and appeared unharmed. I gave a quick prayer of thanks, peeled off my sopping-wet clothes, and all but jumped into the fire seeking its warmth.

When all eleven of us were again gathered, we moved downriver a short distance to find a campsite and to make an assessment of our losses and damages. We were missing three paddles, a sponge, two sets of maps, and two rain jackets. The loss of the paddles put us one short. On the damage end, John's wood-and-canvas canoe suffered a cracked gunwale and some broken planking. All three aluminum canoes were fine. While John sent two fellows out to search both shores for paddles, the rest of us set up camp and prepared a makeshift brace for the crippled side of John's canoe.

About an hour later, the paddle searchers came ashore singing and shouting. They had found all of the missing paddles, one set of maps, and a sponge. All in all, we were indeed fortunate. Though most of our clothing and a lot of our food was now soaked, no one was injured. We built a huge fire to dry out our sleeping bags and ourselves as much as possible.

We tried to maintain a genuine spirit of good cheer, but John and I were both silently calculating the cost of our delay. The consequences of our dumping at Nine Bar Rapids forced us to stop twenty-five miles short of our goal for the day. We no longer had any cushion of time to offset delays. That had all but evaporated while we were bushwhacking our way to Big Sand Lake. The headwinds on the big lakes had also slowed us down considerably. It was Sunday afternoon, and our chances of getting to Churchill in time for the Thursday night train were looking mighty bleak. There was a lot of river left to run before we would get to tide-water. Our original plan did not include paddling on Hudson Bay all the way to Churchill. However, we would still need to travel several miles along the tidal flats from the mouth of the Seal River south to our arranged pick-up spot, at a hunting lodge on Dymond Lake just inland from the tidal flats. The lodge owner would connect with us there and fly us all to Churchill. We would have to wait at the mouth of the Seal River until we had a high tide in order to make our way out around hundreds of boulders and to clear the mud shallows of the river delta. The boulders and shallows preclude the landing of a floatplane at the river mouth. Our group could safely paddle on Hudson Bay only if the weather was clear and the water fairly calm. Those were two conditions the alignment of which we had not seen at all.

When morning came, the only thing that seemed more sullen and somber than our collective mood was the weather. The gravity of our situation was pressing full weight against all of us, and the skies were not the slightest bit sympathetic. No one was doing much talking. We were running short of time. In spite of the care we had taken in the packaging of our food before leaving home, much of it was now soaked. What remained would not be sufficient for more than a day or two beyond our original time frame. Most importantly, though, we were running out of warmth. With some sixty miles to go before reaching tidewater, all eleven of us were now dreading the larger rapids for fear of an upset. We portaged a few of the runs and used painter lines to rope the canoes down still more. John had to take extreme caution and baby his injured canoe. We were now nearing the barrens, and firewood was becoming scarce. It was unseasonably cold. The wind was cruel, and the weather was coming straight in from Hudson Bay. A repeat of the previous day's mishap could mean hypothermia and possibly death.

For much of the day, the headwind on the river made it impossible to tell what has wave and what was current.

We gathered at lunchtime and got a small but cheerful blaze going by burning green willow branches. What really served to cheer us was the sight of several seals swimming in the current near us and hauling out on rocks.

It took us until dark to progress thirty-two miles. The wind made the last four miles seem to take an eternity. We hit the tents after a quick, light meal, each of us exhausted and quite discouraged. It now seemed certain that we would be late in getting to Dymond Lake. We had to try to prepare ourselves for a few additional long, hard days traveling with a minimum of food. John made certain each crewmember was fully aware of both our predicament and our plan. The trip was no more a game of pleasure. That clear fact cut me right to the bone. We were at the point of this river trip where each of the eleven in our group should have been ecstatic, anticipating the final run to tidewater and the joy of achievement. Running the whitewater from this spot to the river's mouth should have been a sensational high and a full-blown rapids rodeo. Instead, full-blown trepidation replaced the joy that might have been. That had me seething inside, and I felt that each of us was being sorely cheated by the elements after all we had been through together. The rain, the cold wind, and the river itself were all indifferent to our plight. What any of us felt entitled to mattered not one iota.

Sleep was a stranger to me that night, for there was indeed a war going on in my head. I spent much of the night praying for wisdom and aid in meeting our needs. I tried to get a mental grasp on every possible move we could make. John and the others were no doubt struggling with similar thoughts and doing a bit of praying of their own. I had one basic idea in mind by early morning, and I let it stew a bit trying to view it from all angles.

I decided to get up and set breakfast out for everybody knowing the fellows would be none too eager to leave the warmth of their sleeping bags. We had one full breakfast left, the main course of which was a wet bag of granola with the consistency of damp sawdust. I rationed out the granola eleven ways, made a pitcher of orange drink, and opened a box of what should have been dried fruit. There would be no fire this morning. What wood there was round about was thoroughly rain-soddened. It had taken two paraffin flares to get the previous night's dinner fire ignited.

Breakfast was quick and fairly quiet. The conviviality and good-natured ribbing so characteristic of this group was noticeably absent. Before long, we were out fighting the wind and the waves yet again. After a couple of miles, I finally felt what I had left stewing in my head was ready for another opinion. John was up ahead waiting for all of us to catch up with him. When all of us were gathered, I asked him and the others to consider my proposal. It seemed highly unlikely that we could make it to tidewater today or make it all the way to Dymond Lake in time for our Thursday flight. Being windbound at the mouth of the Seal River seemed a likely scenario, and an uncomfortable one at best. According to the maps, we were presently at the last wide section of the river that was free of rapids.

Here a floatplane could land quite easily. Up ahead, it would be less likely that a plane could land safely. There was air traffic in the area. We had heard and seen helicopters from the Ministry of Natural Resources on Sunday and again on Monday afternoon. There was a large esker up ahead from which we might easily be spotted by a plane. We had previously arranged for our pilot to fly upriver and look for us on Friday if he had not heard from us by then. It seemed safer, warmer, and less energy-depleting to stay put and try flag down a plane than to push on with an extremely limited amount of food and warmth.

So, sadly, I proposed that we stop. I then waited while everyone had a chance to think this through and voice his opinion. We took a vote after a long and quiet pause, and the vote was for stopping. We would not make it to Hudson Bay. Our trip would end here, after more than 330 miles. Saddened and bitterly disappointed, we headed for the esker and made camp near it on the east side of a small island out of the wind. Only after we set up camp and were all safely off the river did it dawn on me that the date was August twenty-third, my twenty-second birthday.

We spent most of the remainder of this chilly Tuesday catching up on sleep. Gradually, spirits rose and moods brightened. John made a touching gesture, remembering the bottle of Hudson Bay Scotch he had packed along to be opened and shared once we reached tidewater. The label was now indecipherable. So, he re-designated this libation as Big Sand Lake

Scotch. We all toasted each other, our having made it through many days of bushwhacking, and our having come so far with so much ugly weather dumped upon us. It was a kind move on John's part. However, much of the scotch was thrown on the fire, it being an acquired taste most of this group had not yet acquired. The stuff made pretty fine lighter fluid. All eleven of us were well enough now. All we had to do was sit tight and wait.

Ironically, the following day was sunny and relatively warm. For the entire trip, this was the second full day with no rain. Sleeping bags, tents, clothing, and people all got a good drying. We took the three aluminum canoes and our large colored tarp around the island to the esker. There we propped the canoes bottoms up and stretched out the tarp in an effort to make our site as visible as possible. Each of us took shifts manning this site in an effort to spot and flag down an aircraft to get a message to our pick-up pilot.

Ministry helicopters were once again in the area conducting some sort of project work. One chopper flew above our camp but seemingly missed sight of us all together. Then, along about sunset, a small float-plane made a low pass, circled, and landed. We were ecstatic. This fellow had left Churchill and was headed for the First Nation settlement on Tadoule Lake. Our pick-up pilot had asked him to keep an eye out for us, and he had spotted us easily enough. We gave him a section of one of our maps showing our exact location and attached a brief note explaining our situation. This fellow promised to contact our pilot by radiophone from Tadoule, and he assured us we would get our pick up the next morning if the weather in Churchill permitted flying. Things were starting to turn our way, and it looked like we would be boarding the Thursday night southbound train after all.

Expecting to be in civilization soon, we prepared most of the remaining food for supper. This was an odd but filling mishmash feast consisting of freeze-dried vegetables, white sauce, and several pudding desserts. We were just about out of groceries and hoped the fish would be biting. Each of us was ready to return to society; though, because of the way we looked, I doubted that society would be ready for the likes of us. We were a grubby lot, each of us riddled with bug bites, reddened by windburn, and long over-due for a rendezvous with a bar of soap.

We ushered in the new day with a collective groan. The weather had gone sour once again, a pattern of windy drizzle we now considered normal. As one of the fellows put it: When somebody tells you to stick it where the sun don't shine, they must mean northern Manitoba. We suddenly heard a plane about mid-morning. A large Twin Otter floatplane passed right over our heads and began to circle. We raced to meet it, but the pilot merely tipped the wings in salutation and made a beeline toward Churchill. Hugely disappointed at first, we later conjectured that though the aircraft was likely large enough to take all or most of us out in one trip, it was too large to land safely at this spot in the river. The pilot must have figured the water was too shallow.

We gathered ourselves and all of our gear at the esker and watched for both a break in the clouds and for the white Cessna Skywagon that was our pick-up plane. We saw neither. The hours slipped away, and it became bluntly apparent that we would miss the train and would be forced to wait in Churchill for the Saturday evening southbound.

The weather got worse. There would be no flying out today. Getting out on the river in this mess to do some fishing did not seem like a particularly sane idea. We fixed a meager meal of pudding mix and dreamed of sirloin and baked potatoes. I was quite weary of staring at the ceiling of my tent and listening to the patter of drizzle drops hitting the canopy. My tent was in a good spot to be noticed by any plane but in an awful spot with regard to weather protection. Finally, I had to anchor all the guy ropes with large stones, but I was grateful to be horizontal. I had wrenched a muscle in the small of my back while bobbing about in Nine Bar Rapids, and it hurt to bend.

We woke shortly after dawn to the sound of an aircraft engine. When I stepped out of my tent, I immediately ducked, thinking this pilot was trying to part my hair with his Cessna. He came in low and fast. We scrambled to break camp and pack our gear. The pilot told us he had been socked in all the previous day and was stretching regulations by flying now. Regulations be damned. We were mighty happy to see him.

It took three trips to fly the lot of us out to Churchill. We left the three aluminum canoes, as it would cost more to fly them out than to replace them. The plane had weight limits we were not about to stretch. The pilot figured he could probably fly them out another time and put them to use at his hunting camp. I was on the last flight out, and it surprised me how hard it was to part with the river. From the air, the terrain below was a crazy quilt of hundreds of small lakes and barren muskeg patches. Soon we spied the mouth of the Seal River spilling into Hudson Bay. That tugged mightily on my heartstrings, and I immediately made a vow to return.

John booked us into two stark but adequate rooms at the Beluga Hotel. One was equipped with a tiny kitchen. He and I took an empty packsack to the town's grocery store, stocked up, and prepared a feast. Never was there a meal so fully appreciated or so thoroughly devoured. We made use of the hot showers available at the town center complex, and they went a long way to restoring in each of us a sense of being human once again.

I remember being wide awake in the dark on the floor in my sleeping bag. While trying to ease my back muscles, I sent up a few silent prayers of thanks. An awareness started trickling into my brain. Somehow it came to me that I was not really at the end of anything. I was at a threshold with many grand adventures ahead of me.

As I look back on this first Hudson Bay trip after nearly forty years, the lessons learned seem simultaneously hard-won and elemental. It is always far safer to rely on knowledge than upon luck. It takes time to develop the skill sets necessary to travel safely and with confidence. The wild and remote rivers we chose to explore could be unforgiving. Sometimes they demanded a toll. The nature of our journeying meant that mistakes would be made and risks would be required. Our naïveté may have bordered upon foolhardy. Still, each one of us experienced a great deal of personal growth on this journey, and I will not look upon this trip with regret. I think of this set of experiences as the seminal shakedown trip that allowed us to find our balance and thereby assure the success of each subsequent trip.

While sorting through maps not long after our group returned to the Twin Cities, John discovered an unfortunately mislaid note. It was a warning regarding the substantial ledge at Nine Bar Rapids from a trip leader who had lost a canoe there the previous summer. Of the eleven members of this first *Pays-d'en-Haut* Seal River trip, seven of us returned two summers later to successfully traverse the same route. On our second attempt, we made it to Hudson Bay. We budgeted more time, brought considerably more food, and packed along a camping stove. We traveled earlier in the summer and were blessed with far better weather. Beluga whales swam under our canoes at the mouth of the Seal River. We were surprised and elated by their nearness. They journeyed with us for a short while as we headed south toward Dymond Lake. Perhaps their presence was driven merely by curiosity. I choose to interpret their playfulness as an intimate welcome. I had crossed the threshold and would never again be entirely elsewhere.

Serendipity

THE WELL-SEASONED paddle tripper is of necessity a keen planner, an obsessive maker of lists, and a compulsive stickler for details. Such an individual is typically on edge and a true pain in the tuchus immediately prior to trip departure. Most of the hard-bitten paddlers I have met see themselves in this description. The payoff for injecting such stubborn single-mindedness when prepping for a trek comes in the form of self-assurance. Having checked and rechecked everything thrice, you are able to enter the wild reasonably secure in the knowledge that whatever is missing from your kit was deemed unnecessary and intentionally jettisoned long before you ever reached your jumping-off place. Without feeling too smug, you can permit a certain glow of contentment, having once again refashioned yourself into a confident, self-contained nomad.

Try as you may, though, you simply cannot rehearse spontaneity. Whatever degree of competence you possess at outfitting your wilderness experiences, you would do well to always allow room for serendipity.

My longest canoe trip was also one of the most carefully planned excursions I have ever experienced. It simply had to be. Paddling for six weeks without any resupply of food or gear required some mighty careful packing and lots of attention to logistics. Once again, John Edmundson took the lead in putting this trip together. He made certain each of the eight of us was highly involved with the pack-out process and was well aware of the contents of each Duluth pack prior to our departure for the *Pays-d'en-Haut*. I was part of his group of eight friends paddling from Brochet, Manitoba, all the way to the Inuit village of Arviat on Hudson Bay. We paddled, pulled, and lined our way up the Cochrane River, crossed the vast expanse of Nueltin Lake, and ran the Thlewiaza River all the way to tidewater.

Although most of our group had previously paddled on Hudson Bay from the mouth of the Seal River to Churchill, paddling from the mouth of the Thlewiaza to Churchill was completely out of the question due to distance and time constraints. Paddling north to Arviat seemed a viable option. If we met up with a fishing boat and crew willing to ferry us to either community, all to the good. So, we chose to push ourselves all during the trip whenever conditions permitted in order to have a time cushion for paddling Hudson Bay. We knew that once we got there, we would be slaves to the tide and the wind.

It was an amazing trip replete with challenging rapids, grueling portages, ridiculously easy fishing, and merciless squadrons of kamikaze black flies. As we made our way from boreal forest into the barrens, we were all well equipped and well fed thanks to John's attention to detail. He made reservations well in advance for the final leg of our trip. We would take passage—complete with sleeping berths—aboard the slow, all-night train across the muskeg from Churchill to where our van and trailer were stored in Thompson, Manitoba. John purposely left the next-to-last leg of our journey wide open to chance.

There is much in my life that can serve as testimony to the intervention of angels sent from on high to save us from our own ignorance, goofy blunders, or sheer stupidity. Our group was comfortably camped less than a day's paddle south of Arviat and thoroughly windbound. After weeks in the wild, each of us was keenly acclimated to the sounds around us. None of us was at all prepared for the sounds of a half dozen Honda ATVs putting their way south along the tidal flats. Our camp was suddenly inundated with Inuit visitors from Arviat out to do a bit of hunting. These fellows were every inch as startled to meet up with us as we were to encounter them.

We had tea and coffee to offer. Though we were a little concerned about our supply of fresh water, what we had we freely shared. Then we learned a neat trick. One of our guests took up a hatchet and a bucket. He peeled back the top layer of tundra from a patch of ground about a yard square. The permafrost had melted sufficiently in the summer heat to provide a pool of water much sweeter than the brackish stuff we were hauling from a distant creek.

Before long, John had multiple offers to purchase all four canoes once we got to Arviat. They were Old

Town ABS canoes that the fellows greatly coveted for seal hunting on Hudson Bay. Since the canoes were designed without keels, they could easily be used as sleds as ice conditions demanded. None of our guests knew of anyone able to haul the lot of us to Churchill by boat, but we were given the full skinny on regularly scheduled air flights from Arviat southbound. It would be to our advantage to be shed of our canoes before trying to purchase air passage to Churchill, and John now had several eager buyers.

Next morning broke with relative calm near high tide. We wasted no time getting underway, as we wanted to avoid being stranded on the flats shy of landfall at Arviat. Each of us hustled along, anxious to make as much distance as possible before the shallow sea slipped out from under us. Every yard we paddled was one less yard we would have to portage. Mine was the lead canoe at the time. When the water finally gave out, there was only about a quarter mile of mud flat left to negotiate. Footing was better than any of us expected. We portaged the packs first and made a beeline for the shore.

Scanning ahead, our first good view of Arviat told us exactly where to find the airstrip. It was situated between the beach and the village. We would need to portage across the runway before we could get everything assembled at the small building that served as a terminal. Looking behind, I counted heads and canoes and was surprised to see John and his bowman, Joey, stuck more than a mile from shore. Something must have detained them. With the tide fully out, their delay meant a lot of extra hauling across the mud flats. Thankfully, everyone else was bunched together, ready to portage.

It took quite a while before we all came together and learned of each other's adventures. Having hauled their packs to shore, John and Joey had the devil's own time on the return trip trying to determine which one of the hundreds of dark green rocks in the distance was actually their canoe. John was exasperated and just about ready to give up his search. Maybe the high tide would bring his boat to shore. Yes, and maybe God would make it rain down Jack Daniel's Old No. 7, too. Just then, an odd sound remembered from the day before broke into their stillness. An older Inuit fellow with a purely beatific smile putted up on an ATV and offered help. Most assuredly, two grubby white guys stumbling about on the mud flats at slack tide a mile or so from shore must be in need of some form of assistance. Here was John's angel.

While all of this was happening, fellow trip member, Tyler, was doing his best trying to keep me from becoming one with the angels. I had no trouble finding the bright yellow canoe we shared. However, I did seem a bit blinded by the obvious once I started to portage the craft. Tyler suggested in a calm voice that it might be a good idea to wait for the twin-engine plane to taxi past before I proceeded to the other side of the airstrip. I was fine with waiting and thanked him. Air blasts from the props tossed the canoe a bit, but I managed to stand in place keeping it on my shoulders. Seconds later, I raised the bow and was just about to take a step when Tyler hollered, "Stop!"

The plane, which surely would have squashed me like a bug, had executed a quick 180-degree turn and was picking up speed. I set the canoe down, thanked Tyler profusely for saving my sorry hide, and waved sheepishly as the plane hurled past. Maybe it would be safer all around to simply stay in the woods. I was grateful that no guard or airport official came forward to chew me out with the reprimand I deserved. No one said a word to any of our bunch about trespassing.

Turning back toward the beach, a most improbable sight caught our attention. Three men were astraddle a slow-moving ATV with a large green canoe wobbling atop its rear cargo carrier. Some folks just know how to handle a tough portage.

Some while later, after we had made a simple lunch and explored the village, John happily announced he had successfully sold the canoes. He seemed less enthused with our suggestions that he paint his next flotilla hot pink with blaze orange stripes. Flush with cash, John was just about to negotiate the purchase of tickets for our air passage to Churchill when a vintage DC-3 cargo plane landed with a load of building supplies. Think of this aircraft as a flying dump truck. Figuring he had nothing whatsoever to lose, John chatted up the pilot and asked if he would be willing to cut a deal to fly us south.

"Well, technically that ain't at all legal," the pilot replied. "Tell you what. You get your people aboard quick and quiet-like, and we'll give it a go. I can get us in the air before anybody gets snotty and comes around with the rulebook."

"Great," John said. "So, what will this cost?"

"Hell, I don't know," the pilot answered. "I have a little fishing camp way south of here that could use some fixing. A couple hundred bucks would be plenty. How's that sound?"

"Sold!"

"Well then, get your butts aboard. Let's do it."

We took to the sky minutes later. There were no seats in the cargo area and just one small window. We sat on the floor wedged between packsacks, each of us holding tight to the nearest tie-down strap.

A thought struck me, and I turned to share it with the tripmate nearest me. "Do you realize that if the motors conk and we go down, there isn't a soul on earth that knows we are on this plane?"

I received a smile in response. "So, who needs a flight plan, anyway?"

As we rode in the back of a borrowed pickup truck from the airfield into the town of Churchill, I was impressed with John's run of good fortune. I turned to tell him so. "John Boy, it looks like you're golden today," I said.

"You don't know the half of it, Tim," he replied. "Guess where we are all staying tonight."

"It's got to be all eight of us crammed in the last room available at the old Beluga Hotel. Or am I doing first shift for polar bear watch while we camp on the beach?"

"You're not even close," John chuckled. "I met this guy at the Arviat airstrip while you were exploring the village. He's a biologist doing fieldwork up here. He was waiting for a flight to take him north to Chesterfield Inlet. This fellow rents an apartment in Churchill, and it is ours to use for free until train time two days from now."

"Ah, the kindness of strangers," I sighed. "The sweet magic of serendipity."

Zugunruhe

HAVE YOU EVER stood and watched a swirl of starlings in flight and wondered how it is the individual birds never appear to collide with one another? Were human beings to attempt such choreography, I am certain more than a little bumping and bruising would occur. Come to think of it, something along those lines does occur most workday mornings during any given urban commute. How is it that shearwaters, pied wheatears, sandpipers, and monarch butterflies can efficiently assemble and head off en masse to a particular destination thousands of miles away and arrive successfully, while we humans make such a sow's ear out of trying to navigate a supermarket parking lot? What do these creatures possess that most humans appear to lack? This has been on my mind a lot, as I am rapidly migrating toward the winter of my years.

The word *zugunruhe* is of German derivation and a blending of *zug* ("movement" or "migration") plus *unruhe* ("restlessness" or "tension"). Among zoologists, particularly those with a keenness for ornithology, it is a term used in reference to the anxiety animals display when natural rhythms are triggered and the urge toward migration is set into motion. Consider the flipside to the sublime calm of that loon cruising the water just off your campsite at twilight. It comes shortly before the crinkle ice shows up and the first snows of winter frost the shorelines. There is a pulse-quickening frenzy in the air, and if you see a loon at all, it is either noisily ganging up with a few of its buddies to engage in some serious feeding or rapidly passing through alone, heading south. Nothing about the bird sighted at such time brings to mind images of plaintive tranquility. The crispness in the morning air has everything stirring with purpose and determination. Transition is about to occur.

I named the first canoe that was ever entirely my own *Zugunruhe*. At the time of its purchase, almost every part of my life was caught up in a whirl of transition. I had just earned my bachelor's degree at the University of Minnesota and would be starting graduate school there come the end of September. I quit my job at a camping supply store. The lease on my apartment had expired. Except for my new canoe, a blue seventeen-foot Old Town Tripper, everything I owned could fit in the back of John Edmundson's Volkswagen van with much room to spare. John kindly allowed me to store my belongings at his house and graciously granted me the use of his sofa to crash whenever I was in need of shelter more substantial than my tent. Technically, I had no address. What I did have were three precious summer months to go play in the woods before returning to the fury of academia.

First, this canoe of mine would take me to Hudson Bay on yet another *Pays-d'en-Haut* expedition. Next, I would head to Montana for a backpacking trip in the Absaroka Range with a buddy from my canoe camp days. Finally, just as the air would begin to take on that certain autumn crispness, *Zugunruhe* and I would return to Canada. Two friends and I would do a loop paddle trip down the Allanwater and Ogoki Rivers in what is now Ontario's Wabakimi Provincial Park. Here were the makings of a pretty fine season. I had a strong notion that I would be hunkering down to live like a monk for quite a long stretch of time once classes began, and I was driven to get in as much wilderness as would fit into my summer. My experiences would have to sustain me through a double handful of potentially bleak shorebound months come autumn.

Given the manner and location of my upbringing, I could never help being seasonally affected. My parents purchased the wilderness resort that was my boyhood home when I was two years old. From that early age, I have known that summertime and a wilderness setting are for recreation and renewal. The annual migration of fishermen and families seeking refuge from their city selves sparked a flurry within my own family as we rushed to prepare the lodge for yet another busy tourist season. Work, which I first witnessed as my parents' all-encompassing drive to make certain other people were fully enjoying themselves, was inextricable from play. The majority of our lodge guests were actively engaged in the pursuit of a good time and far more inclined to play hard than to spend their precious vacation days with butts rooted to a chaise longue or an Adirondack chair.

As a result of early influences, I have worked toward the fulfillment of a serious commitment to happiness all of my adult life. I play as hard as I work, and summer has always been my season for wildly recreating myself in the image of the little boy inside of me. When I can bring true joy to a task or help generate happiness through group interaction, I thrive, am in constant motion, and contribute much to the success of others. When efforts bog down and become drudgery, it is usually because something or, more often than not, someone has blocked the path to joy. There is rarely subtlety in my body language, as my face faithfully registers what is happening on the inside. Folks who truly know me have all witnessed the high degree of passion and energy I expend on play.

I owned a canoe long before I ever got around to purchasing a car. If that smacks of distorted priorities, all I can claim in self-defense is that several good friends were on hand to help me get where I wished to go. I provided a rich opportunity for friends to do a good turn, and I would like to believe these fine people have in the years since received payment in kind. They earned both my respect and my gratitude. *Zugunruhe* and I traveled many miles together, and that was due in large measure to the kindness of others.

Zugunruhe proved to be an excellent boat for exploring the waters I hungered to know better. Though not entirely indestructible, here was a most forgiving craft that weathered well my clumsiness on portages and my occasional miscalculations in rapids. She was far quieter than the aluminum canoes of my boyhood, and that feature permitted me to paddle closer than I had ever come to waterfowl. Hudson Bay and the rivers pouring into it harbor a vast variety of migrating birds. I was most intrigued by the eiders and the four species of loons encountered on the tidal flats. Molting geese were daily companions and never permitted me to pass by without voicing their displeasure at being temporarily earthbound. For the first few weeks of my wilderness tripping, geese served as alarm clocks. They were always noisily awake long before I wished to rise.

When my gap summer of freedom was near its end, the waters of the Ogoki River turned frightfully cold. My two canoeing companions and I were thankful for the insulating qualities *Zugunruhe* provided with the thick plastic laminate of her hull. Aluminum canoes were never like this. On the riverbanks and at the portages, rose hips burgeoned and became a rich Roma tomato red, always a sure sign that autumn days are approaching. The geese that were molting in July had now gathered to fill the sky with geometry. We lingered around the campfire at twilight, unwilling to let another golden day come to a close. Our student lives would resume all too soon. Harried, compelled, and yielding to forces both internal and external, we would once again migrate away from wilderness.

Once back in the Twin Cities and fully engrossed with coursework, I stowed my tent and moved into a cheap efficiency apartment. I was forced to sell *Zugunruhe* to help defray tuition costs. That stung mightily, but I had little choice. The buddy with whom I had gone backpacking in the Absaroka Range worked at a bank in downtown Minneapolis. He put in a good word for me, and the bank offered me a part-time position. The two of us had spent our time in Montana pretending we were mountain men and reading aloud from Vardis Fisher's account of the life of Jeremiah Johnson around the fire each evening. In true mountain-man style, my friend contacted me when I got the job and cautioned: "Watch yer top knot." Now, in addition to being a full-time grad student, I was working the graveyard shift as a proof operations clerk processing microfiche and becoming a stranger to sleep.

Five semesters later, I was a licensed special education instructor with two lengthy practicums to my credit, a signed teaching contract, and a packsack full of deferred paddle trip dreams. I had scaled an entire mountain range of banking data and was ready to bust loose. A *Pays-d'en-Haut* canoe trip seemed a fine way to celebrate. I joined John as his co-guide once again, and together we led a group of high school students on an exploration of Ontario's Ogoki and Pikitigushi Rivers. Campfires, whitewater, and wilderness excursions formed a powerful, priceless set of bookends bracketing my stint as a graduate student.

In light of my strong play ethic, it may appear at first glance that I chose teaching as my profession simply to ensure my summers would be free. Such is not the case. Given my love of learning and my genuine desire to serve toward the betterment of children, I can honestly say this profession chose me. Nevertheless, the inexorable spirit of *zugunruhe* caught hold of me every spring and every autumn without fail. Just like the plants and the creatures of the far north, I was driven by forces and rhythms far beyond my comprehension to make the most of my time between the summer solstice and the autumnal equinox.

Summer patterns are indelibly written in the script of my life. I always took my teaching duties seriously, but seldom did I use the word "summer" and the word "school" in the same context. At the close of each school year, the echo of the dismissal bell had barely diminished by the time I was packed up and headed back to the good woods. Between paddle trips, I would often help my older brother with his canoe outfitting business, located on Hungry Jack Lake close to where we had both been raised. There was always an ache that came just before Labor Day when it was time once again to leave.

In the late autumn of 1991, just a few months after Maggie and I were married, health conditions greatly affecting my brother's eyesight forced him to sell his outfitting business. Wondering for a short time if we should be the buyers, Maggie and I went north for a final visit. The leaves were gone and so were the loons. The tamaracks had all turned a burnished gold. We borrowed a canoe to take a good-bye paddle down to the palisade bluff at the east end of Hungry Jack. We climbed the bluff and shivered in the wind. I was quietly contemplating the life Maggie and I had just begun together. We were secure with good jobs, good health, good health care, and a comfortable home. It was the joy she brought to children in her classroom that first attracted me to Maggie. Who would have ever thought I would fall so completely for a woman not a part of my paddle trip past? As dear to me as this wilderness had always been, I knew that I loved my wife far too much to ask her to now uproot the life we had started and try to make a living in these woods. Besides, my brother already had a buyer. *Keep dreaming,* I told myself. *Just make certain you use first person plural.*

It began to snow heavily on our return paddle to my brother's dock. Large, wet flakes clung to everything. Maggie's hat, mittens, and coat were caked in white. Still, she kept up her steady, cheerful paddling. The forest was blanketed by the time we pulled ashore. Another transition to a new season had been set into motion. Naturally, that meant a change for all creatures. We would yield, follow the rhythms, and put our trust in each other.

Tendrils

PERHAPS I DO NOT fully possess the secret of happiness. I do know, however, that one of the surest paths to misery is the failure to nourish your passions. If I have learned anything in forty-plus years of paddle tripping, it is this: bridging whatever gulf exists between your work ethic and your play ethic is essential to the healthy maintenance of a happy and purposeful life. I have been as guilty as anyone of compartmentalizing the key aspects of my life, thereby closing off possibilities for joy. The windowless *Dilbert*-style cubicles in which so many of us spend our workdays is a world-class symbol of this closing-off behavior. Office partitions always remind me of the blinders our forebears used to put on their dray horses. I believe each of us becomes much more of a joyful being when we allow tendrils to form, flourish, and entwine the various sides of ourselves. Before the game-over light starts to blink, it makes good sense for each of us to do whatever is necessary to get the connections right.

For years, during my bachelor days as a young special education teacher, I paid little heed to the suggestion that life is far richer when one learns to bloom where one is planted. Rather than embrace the opportunities available to me in the city, I remained, for all appearances, aloof and socially disengaged. There was an odd bit of disjuncture inside of me. My scope on life had become habitual and far too narrow for my own good, for I had taken steps to dichotomize my urban-based occupation from my life as a wilderness traveler. I was governed by the harmful misconception that those two sides of myself had little to do with one another.

I once believed I was initially drawn to itinerant teaching because of the independence inherent to the job. That, however, was not the entire story. Such work does demand a high degree of self-sufficiency. Traveling from school to school and from case to case seemed to offer far greater variety to each workday than always functioning in the same classroom. For a long while, I thrived on the change-up of each school day and the requirement that I be quick on my feet and able to adjust rapidly to altering conditions and circumstances. Due to the wide range of students I served, instructional subject matter could switch from *The Adventures of Huckleberry Finn* to those of Huckleberry Hound all in the course of the same morning. It was good work. For the most part, I loved doing it.

Independence seems a far more palatable term than isolation. The truth is, I have always been crowd-averse. I did most of my teaching one-to-one in a quiet setting. While trying to open up the world to my students one child at a time, I kept myself closed off to much of it. Never have I felt more lost than when my workaday world became all-consuming. The odd thing was, I did not recognize the symptoms until a good deal of damage was done.

Isolation and a dangerous bit of negativity crept in subtly at first. I brown-bagged my lunches because I figured it took far too much time and trouble to arrange anything else. I found early in my career that the faculty lunchrooms of most schools are breeding grounds for gossip, discontentedness, and indigestion. My car was my refuge, my place of solace, and my decompression chamber during each frenetic workday. Being responsible for students in upwards of a dozen schools meant I was generally uprooted, as my schedule was constantly changing. Lunch soon meant wolfing down a sandwich while driving between schools, for my car had also become my office. Because of my hearing loss, I need to be able to see people's faces when speaking with them. Written messages at first, then e-mails, began taking the place of healthy face-to-face human contact with greater frequency. In the interests of time, contacts with my colleagues became clipped, trite, and less frequent. The clock took on a dominant role. I gave less of myself to others in need because I felt too encumbered by my own needs. Where was that peace I felt when paddling not so long ago? Why had that solace become so distant and seemingly unobtainable? Were there no tendrils reaching from one side of my life to the other?

To a large extent, my students were my salvation. I was blessed with the unique situation of working with several of the same children on my caseload year after year. Their lives and activities greatly mattered to me. A small handful of these children were, along with their parents, like extended family. One constant in my instruction was the admonition that life is not a spectator sport, but rather something you had better jump into with both feet. When a couple of my charges began reciting that phrase back my direction, it dawned on me that I must heed my own advice in order to set a good example.

I searched among my teacher contacts and found a writing group that welcomed me as a member. Journaling was a daily ritual and my wellspring for other sorts of creative writing. I got a kick out of writing for the enjoyment of others and discovered a certain knack for it. To help strengthen my ties with colleagues, I volunteered to represent them on our school district's faculty advisory committee.

It surprised me to no end that I could competently address a crowd of special education teachers, along with their administrators, and come away feeling positive.

In short order, I became the chairperson of the advisory committee. Gradually, that stubborn shell I had formed around my city self began to dissolve. Minneapolis is the city of lakes. I took my canoe over to explore several of these, and I found that far more satisfying than simply pining for summer and my return north.

Further inroads toward the shattering of isolation and the creation of tendrils came from surprising directions. I once met six deaf high school students and their two (hearing) leaders at my brother's canoe outfitters. The group had just come off the trail from a week-long trip into the Boundary Waters Canoe Area Wilderness. The kids clearly were having a great time. They were surprised to find in me a stranger able to communicate with them in sign language. The leaders were both in good spirits, but they honestly seemed a bit the worse for wear. Both shared a certain eagerness to get home to a little peace and quiet. This puzzled me until I learned just how this group operated on the water.

Picture an aluminum canoe containing two young, enthusiastic paddlers, both deaf as stones. To get the attention of the bow paddler, the fellow in the stern beats his paddle against the side of the canoe. Vibrations are usually enough to get the desired response. When that fails, a bit of splashed water down the bow-man's neck will certainly serve, and you know where that is going to lead. As both fellows are sign-reliant, they set down their paddles and use their hands to communicate. All forward momentum ceases. Chances are good, though, that both fellows are wearing smiles.

The two trip leaders seemed more than a little frazzled. Their group had traveled less than half the distance originally planned. It took forever just to get across each lake. Noise from repeated gunwale banging still rang in the leaders' ears. That noise had minimized any chance of encountering wildlife. In their own unique way, this was a particularly chatty bunch. It was a good thing the weather was warm and no one wore mittens. I could certainly commiserate. Still, the six young fellows were all obviously high-spirited, safe, and content with their shared wilderness experience. Mission accomplished.

My subconscious self is often occupied with tendril building. It seems mighty determined that I never forget I am an educator as well as a paddler. Most nights in the wilderness, I actually dream about teaching. It has been this way since I left grad school. Have you ever had one of those classic dreams where you are addressing a crowd and look down to discover you are clothed in nothing but your undies? My version has me scrambling to prepare a lesson on quantum physics or fluid dynamics to some snotty little sixth-grade genius infinitely more on top of the subject than I am. I fumble with the textbook, never able to find the correct page. My student becomes a merciless critic, and I am thoroughly humiliated. I have had this dream dozens of times. Thankfully, it now has me chuckling in the morning.

In the final analysis, it took the love of a good woman to save me from myself. Maggie taught kindergarten when I first met her. She was the mainstream classroom teacher for a deaf student I served and case managed. Smitten by the joyful manner in which she interacted with the children in her charge, I soon found myself looking for any reason to be in her classroom. Over the course of five years, we shared a small handful of hard-of-hearing students together. By the time I had prepared the first of these students to start his school year as a fourth grader, Maggie had switched grade levels and was once more his classroom teacher. We figured this was a shared destiny. Our friendship had blossomed quickly, but it took me a long while to build up sufficient confidence to ask for her hand in marriage. Maggie helped me recognize that each of us is a work in progress and none of us can do the necessary work alone.

Witnessing Maggie's strong faith caused me to examine my own. Though I had a good Irish Catholic upbringing, I had pretty much distanced myself from the fold. My experiences as a wilderness traveler strongly affected my views on theology. I felt for a long time that I had more in common with pantheists, animists, even druids than with my fellow Catholics. Maggie's outlook on life helped me to realize that I was as much a child of humanity as a child of nature. With that being the case, I do have an obligation to other people. That obligation requires the creation of greater connection and not greater distance. When I accepted the longer view that Catholicism is also an imperfect work in progress, I was content to rejoin the flock.

God has seen fit to playfully place an amazing web of tendrils into my life, joining its many vagaries. Though I have not always been cognizant of the myriad interconnections, I have to admit I greatly admire the Creator's attention to detail. It delights me that Christ chose a handful of simple fishermen to be his first disciples. When it comes to the work of fishers of men, I trust the Lord is keen on tendrils and is not at all a catch-and-release angler.

Ursine Encounters

W HEN I WAS SIXTEEN and finishing my first summer working at a canoe camp, I took a canoe, borrowed a small tent, and did a solo overnighter before heading home to start the school year. My intention was to camp just off Stairway Portage next to the waterfall that pours into Rose Lake, one of the prettiest spots on the east side of the Boundary Waters Canoe Area Wilderness. However, I arrived to find the campsite already occupied by a group of four paddlers making their way from Ely to Grand Portage along the Canadian Border Route. We chatted for a while. This had been a layover day for the group, and they had done well fishing. As I was traveling light and alone, this foursome said they would not mind my setting up camp on a nearby rock ledge. This was a great kindness, for it saved me from having to portage and head down the lake to find another site.

A campfire would have been great company, but space on the ledge was pretty well maxed out once the tent was up, with corners and guy ropes secured to trees. Besides, I had sandwiches and cookies in my packsack and no need to cook. Smoke from my neighbors' camp wafted my direction. Any nose could tell that fresh fish was on their evening menu. I was enjoying the view of the lake in the pre-twilight and was partway though my second sandwich when a clamor of shouts and pan-banging rose from next door. There was no mistaking what that meant: bear trouble.

Quickly scarfing the rest of my supper, I trotted over to my neighbors to help chase the bear out of the area. If we could persuade this bruin to head east and not return, that would be all to the good. My ledge camp was immediately to the west of my neighbors and sit-uated just above the waterfall. The creek between their site and my own had a log footbridge spanning it. The bear was stubborn. It returned twice in less than twenty minutes and finally departed after being pelted in the rump with a couple well-pitched stones. That was not a good sign, for it meant the creature was habituated to this particular campsite and associated it with food. This was a popular spot, and this bear had likely expe-rienced easy pickings here on previous prowls. I imag-ined the aromas of fried fish and potatoes had proved especially tantalizing.

After accepting a cup of tea as thanks for helping, I wished the foursome happy trails and headed back across the footbridge. In the final light of the evening, I checked my camp for any food crumbs or litter bits that could become bruin bait and hoped my neighbors had done the same. Just what had they done with the fish guts? That question kept me awake just long enough for me to realize there was nothing whatsoever

I could do about it. Then, cinching the top of my mummy bag, I drifted off to the Land of Nod.

It was way past midnight when a new round of pan-banging, shouts, and swearing yanked me right out of a dream. My neighbors seemed like fine folks, but this time they would have to manage on their own. I sat up in the tent and tried hard to listen. Would I even be able to hear a bear splashing through the creek if it headed toward my camp? The footbridge was pretty narrow. Would it be too narrow for this bruin? I opened the tent door, reached for my packsack, and gave it a good sniff. Then, trying to adjust to the dark, I rummaged through its contents, rewrapping everything as best I could. I sure could not detect any food odors through layers of plastic bags and canvas packsack. Still, a bear's sense of smell is excellent and far better than that of any human.

I had just convinced myself that all a body could do now was to stretch out again and try to catch another forty winks when the floor of the tent began to slide and pull taut to one corner. Then I felt a large presence leaning into the left side of the tent. I gave a yell and whacked the tent wall as hard as I could. My fist found purchase. The bear took off, but not before running into a corner guy rope a second time and totally ripping out the tent floor.

Well, that was enough for this boy. Though stumbling around on a ledge in the dark may not be the sanest activity, I was not about to linger. My kit was minimal and did not include a flashlight. Quickly and with a few muttered curses, I untied all the guy-rope knots and stuffed what was left of the tent into my packsack. My eyes had adjusted well enough to the dark to permit me to find my way to the Duncan Lake end of Stairway Portage, where I had stashed the canoe. Tripping over a tree root was likely a greater hazard than bumping into the bear at this point. I wondered if the creature was stubborn enough to circle back and try once again to hit my neighbors' camp.

It is funny how darkness seems to trigger in people a perceived imperative to keep silent and to move about with stealth. I had the canoe loaded and launched and was all but holding my breath trying to keep quiet before realizing there was no one at all within earshot. I paddled for a while, gazed up at the stars, and tried to figure how long it would be before the sun rose. Dealing with the bear was one thing. Placating my fellow canoe camp employee, the owner of the trashed tent, might prove even more of a trial. The guy was a bit of a jerk. He had no idea that I was the one who had given him an entire slab of Ex-Lax disguised in a Hershey Bar wrapper the night he came into the canoe camp totally drunk and thoroughly obnoxious. He had made a true ass of himself. Sure, it was a nasty thing to do, for the effect my little treat had was far more than one might anticipate. I chuckled at the memory. Call it just desserts.

Dealing with the tent and its owner, however, was not an immediate issue. All would look far better in the light of day. Then, moving over to left shore, I tied the bow painter line to a cedar tree. With my life jacket for a pillow, I stretched out on the bottom of the canoe and was soon fast asleep.

On the *Pays-d'en-Haut* canoe trips John and I led together, it had never been our practice to suspend a food pack from a tree branch as a bear deterrent. Bears are superb climbers. Moreover, even a bear of very little brain has the capacity to unfasten your best knots with its teeth. The *Pays-d'en-Haut* practice was to always try to keep as clean a camp as possible. Typically, no one would head off to the tents for the night until all the food was wrapped and packed, all the food packs were closed and placed together, and a rain tarp was secured tightly around the entire works. We set pots and pans atop the tarp to alert us of any unwanted night visitors. This system served us well. Mind you, though we certainly did paddle through wilderness areas inhabited by bears, our trips tended to go to areas rarely frequented by people. The routes we chose were all well to the north of the heavily used Boundary Waters Canoe Area Wilderness and in places where bears with no access to garbage typically avoided humans.

You could argue that taking a small dog into the boreal boonies is just asking to have it end up as an ursine hors d'ouerve. John's longhaired dachshund was a frequent *Pays-d'en-Haut* canoe trip member. Here was a canine of very little brain. John named him Wagi, a shortening of *wagi peegi kewano*. The phrase means "little crooked tail dog" in Anishinaabe. Wagi was cute, inquisitive, stubborn beyond belief, and a whole lot of fun. I remember helping to pull porcupine quills from Wagi's muzzle a time or two, but he and the black bears generally stayed clear of each other.

There were times when this dog came mighty close to being skinned alive and fed to the bears. Wagi was an early riser. When John let him out of the tent in the morning, Wagi would go water a bush and head out on squirrel patrol. This typically meant incessant barking after he had chased a squirrel up a tree. Wagi was an all-too-effective alarm clock, and soon every trip member was awake and stirring. Usually the first one out of the canoe when we came to a portage, Wagi would run back and forth along the trail several times, as if spurring us onward while we hauled the canoes and packs. He was often underfoot but always managed to avoid getting squished. Of course, all his running about meant he crashed heavily when it was time to go to bed. Wagi was too tuckered out one evening to bother with his usual bush-watering routine. He decided it was easy enough just to stay inside the tent, curled up in John's down sleeping bag, and take a pee there. I thought John was going to kill him on the spot. Bad dog, indeed.

Wagi's successor was a chunky little dachshund named Misty. She had a sweeter temperament and was a good deal more sedate than Wagi. Misty would typically jump into a canoe and sack out atop the softest Duluth pack she could find. She stayed clear of porcupines. There was one particular morning when we were especially glad she stayed clear of bears.

Timothy McDonnell

Polar bears are frequently sighted along the shores of Hudson Bay. Churchill, Manitoba, the community where several *Pays-d'en-Haut* canoe trips ended, is located on Hudson Bay, smack dab in the heart of polar bear territory. Just to the south of Churchill along the coast are denning areas used since time immemorial. When a new litter of cubs is born, the bears from the last round of birthing are sent on their way to fend for themselves. They head north, right through the town and right along the tidal flats.

Misty was along on our *Pays-d'en-Haut* Seal River trip the summer of 1985. Having run the river to tidewater, our group paddled along Hudson Bay for two days so as to reach the southbound train at Churchill. We ran out of daylight on our way to Churchill and ended up camping right outside the stone walls of Fort Prince of Wales. The long stint of paddling and dealing with the tides left us exhausted, and we all slept soundly. Thankfully, that included Misty. We climbed atop a wall of the long-abandoned fort at sun-up to take a look about and saw a polar bear at the opposite side of the fort, heading north away from our camp. Given the structure of the fort and the topography of the site, this bear had to have passed right through our camp while we were asleep. We found paw prints in the sand that showed this was indeed the case. Had Misty been awake at the time of the bear's passing, there could have been some serious consequences. A dog chased by a bear will run back to its master.

Making light of the situation once we knew we were safe, our group surmised that we all smelled too bad for the bear to want anything to do with us. We quickly broke camp and headed to Churchill. The local authorities gave us a major tongue-lashing for camping at the fort. One officer had been watching for bear activity and had his binoculars trained on us for much of the morning. We put Misty on a leash, made the short portage to the train depot, and prepared ourselves for an abrupt re-entry to the less wild side of our lives.

In July of 1999, I joined three friends for a canoe trip down the Asheweig River in northwestern Ontario. Tom, Big Mike, and Swegle were paddle trip comrades of long standing. In my trip journals, I always referred to them as "the usual suspects." We took a floatplane from the tiny community of Pickle Lake and put in near the east end Shibogoma Lake. To look at Shibogoma Lake on a map and to trace your pencil or finger along the route of navigation to the point where the Asheweig flows out necessitates several zigzags. Big Mike said the lake reminded him of his E.K.G. readout. We only had to navigate the last few miles of this lake before heading down the river. Our pull-out spot was on the north end of Sourdough Lake. This was not a great distance. However, there were plenty of fun rapids along the route and decent brook trout fishing to boot. As always, we found more than enough to keep us occupied and happy.

To the south and a little east of where we were pad-dling is the Anishinaabe village of Webequie, on the shore of Winisk Lake. People of this First Nation com-munity had made an attempt at a business venture building camps in the bush to hire out to hunting and fishing parties. One of their camps was on the river-bank just a little upstream from Straight Lake. There was no one about when the four of us pulled in to look things over and to stretch our legs. It did not appear as though anyone had been there for some time, judging by the vegetation grown up around the buildings. There existed two bunkhouses and one kitchen build-ing. All the buildings were unlocked. All of the stovepipes had been removed, leaving three gaping holes to the sky. This I found particularly odd. Even more peculiar was the dead hooded merganser drake someone had left on the floor of the kitchen building. There were two broken eggs on the counter.

Tom speculated that someone had deliberately tried to bait bears so as to have this camp trashed. What else would explain such a bizarre act as leaving a dead duck on the floor? Swiping stovepipe seemed a rather low blow, also. We had no idea what sort of so-cial dynamics had led to this apparent attempt to ruin a camp. All we wanted was a clear spot to set up our tents and to cook supper.

There were several dried-up fish carcasses in an otherwise clean area down along the shore. A bit of work to tidy up the spot yielded a fine camping site. Before long, Swegle had a fine chicken and pasta supper going. He has always been an absolute wizard at whipping up one-pot delights. I have never been able to fathom this man's patience when it comes to dinking around with the two Primus camping stoves we always used on our trips together. I would have converted both of these damned fussy little cookers into canoe anchors long ago. He and Tom were always able to manage some kind of voodoo incantation that kept the stoves alive. I had to admire that.

On toward sundown, Big Mike looked across the bay and spied what he thought was the first moose of the trip. However, binoculars confirmed that our first moose was actually a very large black bear heading straight for our camp. We were downwind from this bruin and as far as we could discern, it had not yet caught our scent. At Tom's insistence, we quickly packed up all our food and dishes into the canoes and headed out to the bay. There was no argument.

I was honestly surprised at this reaction from the fellows. I wondered what made this creature any more of a threat than the typical Boundary Waters nuisance black bear. Those bruins were usually easy enough to persuade to leave. Tom gave me a blunt reality check. "Persistence," he said. He and Big Mike had run into a couple of problem bears one summer while staying at fish camps on the Winisk River. The bears had become accustomed to hitting the fish camps and simply would not go away. Shouting and banging pans together got you nowhere with such a habituated bruin. It took the additional persuasion of a shotgun, and that was one item we did not have in our kit on the Asheweig. To have this bear amble through one of our tents or trash a *wanigan* looking for food certainly would have soured our experience. After some discussion, we decided to clean up camp, pack up the tents, and move over to the larger of the two bunkhouses for the night. By the time we got settled into our new digs, there was no sign of Bruno. He had apparently passed right on by, well behind the camp.

Before we packed up and continued down the river the next morning, I poked around the camp a bit. I liked the way the bunkhouse we slept in was constructed. It was obviously built by someone who cared about doing a quality job. Back in the bush a bit was a simple log structure that I took to be an icehouse. There were no windows, and a layer of sphagnum moss about a yard deep covered the dirt floor. What once had been a serviceable axe rusted in the dirt near the icehouse with its handle rotting. That sort of neglect is something I have never understood. Four or five fine freighter canoes were stacked behind the smaller bunkhouse. Their hulls were fiberglass rather than the traditional wood and canvas. They represented a substantial investment on someone's part. There was an older freighter with a busted bottom rotting back in the underbrush next to an enormous pile of trash. More bear bait.

A few spent shotgun shells and a considerable amount of graffiti explained that goose and duck hunting were primary purposes of the camp. The latest recorded date on the wall of the larger bunkhouse was from 1995. Whoever constructed the camp appeared to no longer maintain it. Moreover, somebody appeared hell-bent on undermining whatever enterprise had been established here. Though it was none of my affair whatsoever, I quietly cleaned up the egg mess in the kitchen and buried the carcass of the merganser drake back by the trash pit. I was filled with disgust as I pondered the way people go to such absurd lengths to be ugly and cruel to one another. The clean-up I did out of respect for the duck. I felt truly sorry for the bears. They act upon impulse, and unlike human beings, cannot do otherwise.

Not long ago, a public interest segment on a Sunday morning news program caught my attention. It was about efforts to control unwanted bear activity at Yosemite National Park. Included was footage of bears crawling through open car windows going after food left on car seats. Nope, the National Park Service has not yet outlawed visitor stupidity. The segment made it clear that this type of activity is fairly common in our more popular wilderness parks. In an effort to minimize the negative consequences of ursine encounters, bruins are being captured, ear-tagged, and fit with radio collars for tracking purposes. To my way of thinking, that is all truly unfortunate. It significantly alters our definition of wilderness. Wild creatures are made considerably less so in our efforts to manage them. Since most of us have no clue at all how to interact with anything truly wild, we leave it to the authorities to come up with some form of control when creatures become inconvenient.

After watching the segment, I went searching for a photograph Swegle took on one of our canoe trips. This showed a large black bear on the bank of the Bloodvein River feeding on the hindquarters of a moose. We rounded a bend and came upon this scene quite suddenly. As we were downwind, we were able to watch for several minutes from our canoes before the bear became aware of our presence. The moose was likely a winter kill that collapsed at the river's edge. It was plenty pungent. The bear's muzzle and chest were covered with the gore of its feeding.

Here, then, was recycling the way nature intended. No garbage dump. No car windows. No trashed tents. No unhappy tourists. The bear took off for the bush when it finally spotted the four of us. I feel quite certain it returned to its meal a short time after we had paddled on and cleared the area. I also feel there is room enough in the wilderness for all, provided we are humble enough to acknowledge that humans are not always the ones in control.

Trout Flies and Black Flies

L AYOVER DAYS ON a paddle trip are precious gifts of unstructured time, and who among us desires less of that? It was an uncharacteristic bit of jealousy on the afternoon of one particular layover day that launched my entry into the world of fly angling. I would sincerely like to believe that I do not have an envious nature. A tripmate can bring on a paddle trek any manner of gadget or gizmo. I can admire it and give it an appreciative nod without becoming at all covetous. However, nothing shades me a jealous green faster than witnessing in passing or from the sidelines another person fully engaged in an experience I would thoroughly enjoy.

Activity envy flared in July of 1993, on my first of several canoe trips with the trio of friends I respectfully refer to as "the usual suspects." Tom, Big Mike, Swegle, and I were near the midpoint of our trek down the Clearwater River in northern Saskatchewan. We stopped to spend an afternoon fishing at the confluence of a tributary. There was a pretty waterfall here at the end of a stream that drained Careen Lake. There was also a group of four men fly-fishing for Arctic grayling with what seemed to me far too much ease and success. They had flown into Careen Lake for the sole purpose of fishing, and they were absolutely hammering the grayling using tiny black gnat trout flies.

Yes, we managed to pull in one or two of these iridescent piscatorial beauties ourselves, but the grayling obviously preferred the gnats to the larger spin tackle we were chucking. Moreover, to avoid tactlessly encoaching upon the pool to which this foursome had previous claim, our group members either headed upstream or got relegated to the pool's less productive far margins. There was enough humanity in our group to congratulate the foursome on their tremendous success, but just barely. They sure looked like they were having fun hooking up solidly on about every other cast. It was excruciating to watch.

A couple of summers later, our group of four put in at Selwyn Lake just across the Northwest Territories border with Saskatchewan to paddle the Porcupine River. We hauled out at the first rapids to try our luck fishing. Tom pulled a case from his personal pack and strung up nine feet of graphite fly rod. The rest of us were chucking spinners and spoons just as we always did. Tom began to take more fish than the rest of us combined, and it was painfully obvious he was having a grand time doing so.

That did it. Three of us took fly-casting lessons together upon our return to the Twin Cities. Swegle spent part of the winter building his own fly rod. Our subsequent canoe trips found each of the four of us packing his own fly-fishing gear and relishing the few hours we set aside for casting for brook trout and Arctic grayling.

More often than not, layover days on our northern river trips were days spent weather-bound. This was particularly true on our Kazan River trip in July of 1997.

Good weather days were always paddle days. As ever, we were up against time constraints with miles to make. Therein lies the rub for the paddler with a passion for fly-fishing. When the wind is howling enough to keep you off the river, just how sane is it to wade mid-stream and try to cast trout flies? When the sky starts popping, it is best to remember that nine feet of graphite makes one mighty effective lightening rod.

It takes several weeks to paddle the entire Kazan River from its source near the sixtieth parallel to its terminus at Baker Lake. We had ten days. Selecting a section of the upper river that seemed a good match for our collective interests, we flew into the site of an abandoned weather station on Ennadai Lake. Our takeout spot was on Angikuni Lake, about 130 miles downriver.

The four of us carved our fly-fishing time from the calm of a few stolen moments in the quiet of the dawn. We were sometimes able to get in a little casting by taking advantage of whatever stillness came our way before we hit the tents and settled in for the night. Windless weather is not a prerequisite for productive fly-fishing. However, it certainly is a preference. There is much joy in being able to spot fish in clear water, to watch them rise and feed, and to fool them into taking your imitation. Mind you, as much as each of the four of us cherished calm weather coupled with quiet time spent casting flies to hungry fish, we were begging for steady winds. We welcomed any breeze that would give us a reprieve from the merciless hoards of voracious black flies.

The Kazan River courses through vast tundra plains surprisingly diverse in berries, mosses, and wildflowers. Once the shroud of snow and ice has melted, the pace of all life on the tundra shifts into overdrive. This exhilarating pulse can have an amazing effect on those who witness it. Experiencing it firsthand is worth a great deal. Yes, that includes putting up with the bugs. Never in my many years as a paddler have I felt so free as when journeying through this raw, unpolished, and wonderfully wild environment. Never have I found a hike so liberating as when exploring the eskers that cross this broad land like great sand highways. The barrens are anything but bare during the few weeks of summer. Birdlife abounds. Daylight dominates, and the increased hours of sun have everything astir. Save for the esker ridges, this land is like one enormous saturated sponge. The topmost layer of permafrost thaws a bit. Water is everywhere, and every little pool is prime habitat for mosquitoes. Black flies breed in moving water, and there is plenty of that.

An optimist will tell you that an abundance of black flies means happy birds and well-nourished fish. Add to this the pleasant fact that black flies help to propagate blueberry plants, and the picture looks almost rosy. A realist scratches his bites and emphatically disavows any redeeming value in the evil little stinkers. That is never more manifest than when the flies are busy making a meal out of you. Black flies are attracted to sweat, body heat, and exhaled carbon dioxide. Some paddlers would add DEET to that list, swearing that bugs favor it as a sort of insect *digestif.*

Canoeing the Kazan River in July means coping with a bumper crop of black flies. That takes a particularly determined mindset and a definite regimen of precautions. Closed collars, tight cuffs, and fine mesh head nets are essential clothing. Gloves keep your hands from turning into hamburger, but they must be removed frequently to re-apply bug dope. Unless there is a strong, bug-scattering breeze in the evening, lounging about after supper is highly unlikely. Hot meals are prepared using gas stoves. Remember, tundra is treeless plain. A small campfire is possible, but only after a significant amount of scrounging for puny willow twigs or rare bits of dry driftwood.

Failure to use extreme caution when entering a tent can jeopardize not only a good night of sleep but also the goodwill of your tentmate. A careless foot can tear out the vital no-see-um-proof mesh barrier of a tent door quicker than you can swat a bug. It can take a good fifteen minutes to kill all the black flies that come into the tent with you on your clothing before you settle down to read or to sleep. You had better want to fish if your tentmate is doing so, because neither of you will want to go through the bug-kill routine more than once an evening.

Tom was my tentmate on our Kazan River trip. We decided one evening that it was time to uncase the fly rods and go tease the grayling a bit. Our campsite was on the riverbank next to a fairly shallow swift. A few

Arctic grayling were finning in the water just upstream from camp. Tails and dorsal fins broke the surface as they fed on an abundance of bugs. Big Mike and Swegle had both retired to the comfort of their tent. Unless they heard us whooping joyously at multiple hookups with cooperative fish, they would not emerge until morning.

I am ashamed to admit that what the two in the other tent actually heard was me cursing a blue streak. Tom was already casting and doing well. I was having the devil's own time constructing a leader and trying to thread tippet through the eye of a tiny trout fly that I could not see at all well. Each time I raised my head net to get a better view for the tasks, black flies went straight for my eyelids. When I removed my gloves to tie knots, the black flies made a veritable casserole out of the back of my hands. To avoid having DEET eat away at my fly line, I had thoroughly washed the bug dope off my hands. That may have been a big mistake. Where was the joy in this? How had Tom managed? It was largely a case of mind over matter. In my case, the black flies had me close to conceding defeat.

I calmed down, finally got everything properly rigged with my fly rod, and stepped into the river. One grayling rose and refused my dry fly. A second soundly smacked into my line. A third connected solidly, but it threw the fly just as I was preparing to bring it to hand. Tom was soon ready to hit the tent. Though my total fishing time was less than ten minutes, he got no argument from me. The grayling could wait. I was thoroughly disgusted with myself and ready for bed. Once the tent was zipped up for the night, our bug-kill ritual commenced with a particularly zealous vengeance.

When morning came, Swegle kindly suggested I take a few casts before I packed away my fly rod. He would handle the breakfast chores. This took me by surprise. Each of the four of us is exceptionally skilled when it comes to ribbing one another. Following my loss of temper and less-than-pleasant language, I felt a snarky bit of ridicule was bound to come my direction. Not so. I waded knee-deep and began to scan the water. There was no wind to chop the surface, and I soon spotted just what I wanted. It took me three casts to connect with a nice, healthy grayling. Giving thanks, I examined its outsized dorsal fin. These always look more like a sail on a grayling than like any type of appendage. I gave it a little time to revive and then respectfully set it free. Content and yet humbled, I certainly was not going to let out a whoop.

It was tempting to tarry wherever the fishing was highly promising. Our compromise during paddle days was to keep our spinning rods rigged and readily accessible. We usually took a short break once or twice each day and fished from the canoes. A strong tailwind near Dimma Lake pushed us along steadily one morning, and we drifted for miles, pulling in fish to our hearts' content. Lake trout on the Kazan were plentiful and delightfully obliging. They eagerly hit the spoons and spinners we cast. Save for the bounty that went toward one fine lake trout meal Tom prepared over a willow twig fire, we released everything we caught.

Making an early stop one afternoon, we set up camp on a pretty crook of riverbank partially surrounded by an esker ridge. A front was moving in, assuring us of snotty weather. The barometric pressure was dropping like a tossed brick. All four of us broke out the fly rods and flogged the water just upstream from camp. We were determined to take full advantage of the feeding fish while conditions permitted. When wind made controlling fly lines difficult, each of us switched to spinning rods. Several small lake trout cooperated, as did a few grayling. Before long, though, we hightailed it to the tents just ahead of the rain. I noticed with a certain smug delight that the wind negated our need for a tent time bug kill.

Morning arrived gray and sour. The temperature had troughed. We were in for an all-day blow with a lot of rain. As was our standard practice, our two tents were pitched within hailing distance of each other. Tom called out the weather status and suggested we stay put. Each of us instantly voiced consent and settled in for a long snooze. Let the rain drown every last bug on the tundra. Let the wind howl and carry each miserable bug carcass all the way to China. This was a layover day.

It seemed ages before the steady tattoo that was making a wet snare drum out of the tent fly diminished to a weak patter of drizzle drops. I had been listening hard for just that shift in sound. Satisfied that it had indeed arrived, I pulled on my rain gear and Wellies and lit out for the high country.

Each of us took solitary hikes from time to time, always with binoculars, and always with an eye peeled for wildlife. My hike began with a *sik-sik*, an Arctic ground squirrel that was digging in a sand bank near our canoes. Skittish, it popped into a hole when I approached. This fuzzy fellow gave me encouragement, for I was not the only creature goofy enough to venture out on such a day. There were tufts of caribou hair on the ground near a willow thicket. At first, I took this to be shed hair. Something about its abundance made me look closer. A few larger clumps had skin attached. This was from a kill.

Our foursome had sighted only a half-dozen caribou thus far on our trip. One was a lone straggler making its way along the shore of Dimma Lake. Five caribou passed behind our campsite one evening when we were preparing supper. A fine bull was in the lead with a rich, dark coat showing just a few signs of shedding. Though we were not witness to the throng of a mass migration, the remnants of caribou were all over the tundra. Sun-bleached vertebrae, shed antlers, and wolf scat comprised of hair were plentiful. To the extent that the flattened moss and compressed ground I crossed on my way to the highest point of land could be called a game trail, it was a trail most certainly created by the passing of caribou.

Twice I flushed coveys of willow ptarmigan. My heart always beats a little faster when that happens, as the birds and I are equally startled. Our group had watched an Arctic fox one morning early in our trip while it was out patrolling the riverbank. I imagined the good hunting that fellow would find in these parts. Think of it the way the fox might: *sik-sik* as a main course with willow ptarmigan for afters. Summer life on the tundra is indeed rich.

This esker ridge appeared to go for miles, roughly parallel to the course of the Kazan. I kept climbing. Looking back toward camp from up top, I could not make out our two tents. The scope of my vision was shortened by the gray scud of fog and drizzle that hung over our portion of the river. The wind was busy carrying off low-slung hunks of cloud like so many torn rags. I kicked over a piece of caribou antler with the toe of my boot. Some critter had once gnawed away at part of it. I set it back into the ground just as I had found it and kept walking. My thoughts tossed back and forth from hunter to prey.

The Kazan River country was not always an unpeopled land. The remains of Inuit encampments have been located throughout the area and studied in depth. Tent rings, *inuksuk* markers, and cairn graves are the only signs left of the people who once belonged here. These were a people that had subsisted on caribou and fish from time immemorial. We had read that their long-deserted encampments were more prevalent north of Angikuni Lake. That did not stop our foursome from pulling ashore and stomping across the tundra on a few occasions to explore rock formations we spotted as we paddled. Though our shore patrol explorations added nothing to anthropological research, I loved the energetic curiosity that set them in motion.

The remnants our group found in the hunting camps along the river all appeared to be of fairly recent origin. These were not hugely abundant but were certainly noticeable. They included bits of rusted tin, pieces of tooled wood, iron stove parts, rubber boot soles, a pair of wooden sled runners, and numerous caribou skulls, each with a single bullet hole. At a couple of sites, a great many caribou bones had been cracked and widely scattered by scavengers. Anything at all edible had been given a thorough gnawing before being abandoned.

Making my way steadily along the esker, I pondered the tough life a caribou undergoes. Black flies are a ruthless plague to caribou. I could certainly relate to that. I could also relate to the way caribou are governed by hunger. Ever in search of food, they are frequently on the move across the tundra to where lichen and browse are in greater abundance. Their transience explained the myriad game trails crisscrossing everywhere. I liked how ubiquitous these trails were and how they often extended for miles along the tops of eskers. It pleased me that the caribou and I both chose the high ground. There was wolf scat in several places on this particular esker. I wondered if wolves were now more consistent hunters of caribou in this area than were the few humans who ventured inland to hunt.

Before making my way back to camp, I hiked down off the esker toward the river. The drizzle had stopped, but wind persisted. Thankfully, it continued to keep the bugs from lunching away at me. A pair of tundra swans with one fuzzy cygnet swam just a short way out from the riverbank. I hoped the cygnet would be spared from ending up some fox's lunch and would grow to become as magnificent as its parents. I thought of the *sik-sik* I had seen at the start of my hike. It likely had a tough time remaining evasive and alive.

Walking along the riverbank with the wind in my face, I at last spotted our two canoes. Our two tents were only a short distance up the bank from the canoes. As I came up through a break in a willow thicket, an Arctic wolf was crossing that distance sniffing the ground and heading toward the river. It was upwind from me. I wanted the others to see it, but there was no time to alert them. Our encounter lasted mere seconds. I was about twenty feet away and standing stock still when the wolf spooked, turned, and ran. It was an impressive creature with yellowish-white fur a bit matted and shabby. It seemed well-nourished, too, kind of on the plump side. I had never been so close to a wolf in the wild. It looked back only once. I followed with my binoculars for a bit, but I lost all sight of it by the time it reached the willows. Who knows what the wolf was after and what drew it into camp? Maybe it was the *sik-sik*. Maybe it was the willow ptarmigan.

The weather finally cleared, allowing us to paddle. However, the temperature took a nosedive. By the time we reached Angikuni Lake, we were far less concerned with the black flies and far more occupied with the business of staying warm and dry. Fortunately, each of us was properly equipped to layer up in the style of the

Michelin Man and deal with the cold. Moreover, it was immensely satisfying to realize that we were experiencing a true bug-killing chill. We would be on our way home well before a next hatch.

As we waited to rendezvous with our floatplane, I began thinking yet again about the people who once lived along the Kazan. Just what would those Inuit of long ago have thought of this journey my three friends and I made simply for the pleasure of exploring? Would they have seen purpose or value in our venture? What might they have made of the way we cast tiny feathered hooks with long sticks purely for the pleasure of capturing fish and letting them go? I grinned when it dawned on me that they might consider our catch-and-release fly angling as nothing more than four fools playing with their food. I asked a blessing for their descendants, then joined the other fellows to help arrange our gear for the flight south.

The four of us spotted a second Arctic wolf before our trip drew to its close. This we saw from the air on our way back to the flight base. As we flew overhead low and loud, the wolf seemed uncertain where to turn and what to make of the roar from our floatplane. We watched as it ran along an esker. I imagined the way it would eventually slow to its hunting trot once the roar had gone and the sense of danger had passed. This wolf would resume its purpose in this place. I envisioned it cruising the same esker game trails I had walked, as free a creature as I could ever hope to be.

One Blade or Two?

KAYAK TRIPPING IS a somewhat solitary activity. It can be as quiet or as musical as you are willing to make it. Even when you are traveling amid a pod of other paddlers, you need only to pull ahead, fall a bit behind, or take a few strokes to one side to be off on your own. There is usually more than enough quiet in my life. That is one blessing that comes from being hard-of-hearing and having hearing aids equipped with volume controls. I do find, though, there is seldom enough opportunity available to reconnect with wilderness solitude. With a head full of music and a soul hungry for the wild, I gravitated to the sport of kayak touring in the summer of 2000. This was not by design but by default.

Maggie was not interested in doing an extended canoe trip with me. She was far more receptive to the kind of experience where you paddle around for an afternoon and then return to a sunny cabin deck for a nice glass of wine. Perhaps I should give that a try some summer. My canoe trip buddies, the usual suspects, were all off exploring other avenues that season. They were either engaged in building projects, occupied with family commitments, or traveling with their spouses. Giving up paddling for a summer until we could all reconvene was not an option I was willing to entertain in the slightest. You might as well have asked me to give up breathing. So, as odd man out, I packed up my car one early July morning and hit the long road north to Pickle Lake, Ontario.

The tiny community of Pickle Lake is about as far north as a highway will take you in Ontario. My paddling pals and I had used this as our jumping-off point for a fun canoe trip down the Asheweig River the summer before. Lynn and Bernie Cox of North Star Air were operating a sideline service in those days called Canoe Frontier Outfitters. The idea of once again using this outfitter and taking an extended solo trek by canoe surfaced just long enough for me to nix it with a combination of equal parts guilt and responsibility. When Lynn expressed in a winter newsletter an interest in offering the option of a guided kayak trip to previous clients, I pounced on it. Lynn's enthusiasm fueled my own. It inspired me to consider how I might adapt a kayak to waters more typically explored by canoe. As I was a novice kayaker, Maggie was far more receptive to the idea of my going with a guide than she had been with my short-lived scheme of doing a solo excursion. I liked the challenge of learning a new sport, especially one involving water and wilderness.

With regard to sports, let me explain something. I am not exactly built like Yao Ming. The inseam on my trail pants is barely twenty-six inches. On the other hand, just like Ratty and Mole, I am the perfect size for messing about in boats. Prior to heading out alone to Pickle Lake, Maggie and I drove up to my mother's home in Grand Marais, Minnesota, so I could attend a two-day kayak clinic on Lake Superior. I learned self-rescue techniques and enough about the sport of kayaking to become irreversibly infatuated with it. With the largest lake in the world at your doorstep, how many incentives do you need before you start to explore? With kayaking, I was blessed to discover there is more than enough to learn and enough enjoyment in the learning to keep me happily engaged for the rest of my life. Moreover, I soon found I could sing to my heart's content while kayaking and disturb none but the loons and the terns.

Does there exist in some archival cache an ancient repertoire of traditional paddling songs for kayakers? I have yet to come across any, and this puzzles me a bit. After all, the French-Canadian voyageurs of the fur trade era were a rather melodious lot, and the kayak does predate the bark canoe in North America by at least 4000 years. The rhythmic dip and swing of my double blade is no less hypnotic than that of a canoe paddle. Each time I am in a kayak, I have plenty of music running through my mind as I bob across the water.

I suspect because a kayak was originally intended as a vehicle for stealth and hunting, music did not come into the mix until the hunt was over. There is such singularity to the craft. It was built for one alone. Using scarce, precious scraps of wood, each Inuit kayak was constructed to the exact dimensions of its owner. It was the *umiak*, or women's boat, where I imagine singing came into the picture. Consider the gregarious nature of a group effort led by purposeful females. In my humble opinion, women are more typically part of what is best in the world. Italian cooking and smiling babies are evidence enough to convince me. Music is in there somewhere, also; but I get ahead of myself.

For years, the joy of my annual canoe trek always commenced with the snarky camaraderie of a grueling road trip shared as a foursome. I was sorely missing that. Music and audiobooks did help take the edge off the miles, as did stopping frequently to stretch and to fill my lungs with spruce-scented air. Dining alone was the most difficult. A little punchy and a bit worse for the wear, I pulled into the parking lot of Pickle Lake's Winston Hotel right about suppertime.

There is plenty of irony round about if you are in the mood to look for it. Irony has been seeking me out for years. Partly out of curiosity, partly in preparation for a trip to Rome and the Amalfi Coast that Maggie and I were planning, the audiobook I was listening to on my long drive was *Bella Tuscany* by Frances Mayes. Vivid descriptions of the Italian countryside, along with recipes and all the ingredients for the sweet life in Italy had me salivating. Imagine my surprise when I discovered it was Italian night at the restaurant in the Winston Hotel. Unfortunately, this particular dining establishment is to Italian gastronomy what I am to the sport of basketball. (Honestly, I could not manage a clean slam-dunk with a large stepladder.) With as much optimism as I could muster, I ordered the lasagna and popped a couple Tums in preparation. Yes, the meal was every bit as lame as I had anticipated.

Having called Chris Taggart of Canoe Frontier Outfitters from a phone booth on the drive north, I spent a little while sorting through my paddling gear before turning in for the night. Chris was scheduled to be my guide and kayak trek companion for the next six days. He had been unfalteringly kind and jovial in our telephone conversations, something that Maggie and I both greatly appreciated. I hit the hay in sweet anticipation of a fun week ahead, hoping the lasagna would refrain from making a midnight encore.

My memory and my journal notes collaborate to bring me back to that initial kayak tripping adventure in a flash of clarity and great fondness. On that first evening deep in the Ontario wilderness, the sky had just enough energy in it to promise some serious post-dusk pyrotechnics. Two kayaks were pulled up for the night and tied fast to trees on a classic slab of Canadian Shield. Two tents were securely pitched, doors rolled back just far enough to allow good ventilation but near enough to close without fuss at the first clap of thunder or the first drop of rain. Two extremely well-sated paddlers, each in his own tent, reflected on the day and listened to the waves lap against the shore. Sleep was mere minutes away. All was well with the world. What this particular paddler had hungered for since pulling ashore from his last paddle trip was happening all about him. Peace was settling in and making a home for itself. It was a magic time comprised of beginnings and reconnections.

When I had finished bringing my journal up to date, the events of the day bobbed joyfully through my consciousness. I thought of my cadre of paddle trip companions and how it had expanded over the years. Chris was certainly a fine addition to the lot. I imagined trying to live on Kraft macaroni and cheese for seven months straight. Chris had done that. I imagined him trying to use this as his body's major fuel in an attempt to paddle and portage some 4,750 miles across Canada. Chris was alone and trying to make his way from Montreal to the Pacific Ocean all in one paddling season. I found it both ironic and refreshing that for all Chris had accomplished as a canoeist, he still had an honest and self-depreciating humor about him. His hat still fit.

I found it ironic that this young fellow, who was tagged with the name The Kraft Dinner Kid by his paddling peers, had set out for the two of us such an incredible supper. Perhaps in a culinary sense, Chris had been trying to make up for lost opportunity. Frances Mayes would surely have been proud. Hors d'oeuvres consisted of prosciutto, cacciatore salami, sliced ham, red and green bell peppers, Colby Jack cheese, Bermuda onion, and herb-seasoned tomato wedges. Supper was a simple pasta with a homemade Bolognese, more ham, and Italian bread smothered in melted Parmesan cheese and garlic butter. I wondered just where this amazing repast had been hiding during the Winston Hotel's Italian night. There was, of course, an excellent wine pairing. With the greatest restraint, we set in reserve half of our bottle of Chianti to enjoy with a fish dinner later in our trip.

Chris created this fine spread using a slick new Primus camp stove and a tiny stovetop backpacker's oven. My meager contribution had been a bit of a sad joke. Chris tossed me a mixed bag of chocolate chips, miniature marshmallows, coconut, and some store-bought sponge cake that had not held up at all well in a kayak hatch. He suggested that I get creative. I thought I was equal to the challenge. The result may have proven otherwise, as the concoction likely entered and exited both of our digestive tracts without any need to change color or structure. If I found any culinary redemption, it was in my preparation of coffee. I brought along a simple French press and a pound each of good Kona and Kenya AA. I found in Chris a fellow java junkie and a highly caffeinated fellow after my own heart.

This first night, our camp was just a bit north of Thurston Bay on North Caribou Lake. Chris and I flew in from the Pickle Lake airfield with both kayaks strapped to the amphibian floats of North Star Air's Cessna Caravan. We had spent most of the morning organizing food and gear. It was essential that we conduct a trial packing of the kayaks while still at the outfitting base. I soon surmised there must be about a thousand different ways to pack a kayak. Balance and keeping a proper center of gravity were the key aims. I soon discovered that the packing procedure for kayak trekking has a lot less of a fudge factor than does its canoe trip counterpart. Long and thin packages worked far better than short and squat. Everything went into watertight immersion bags.

I paused in the packing process to ask about portaging our jumble of waterproof bags. Chris simply smiled and shared that we would likely have just two or three short portages around rapids. He was the very picture of self-confidence, while he calmly tried to assure me that we would deal with any obstacle in whatever manner served best when the time came. No worries.

Both of our kayaks were what Bernie Cox called Tupperware boats. That is, they were made of polyethylene plastic. I greatly appreciated that Lynn and Bernie had taken the trouble to locate a smaller boat for me from a fellow outfitter in Atikokan, Ontario. The kayak fit me perfectly, and save for its hue, I liked it quite a lot. The color scheme was a mixture of yellow and a shade of red the manufacturer called firecracker. This was a somewhat unfortunate blend that reminded me of nothing so much as a long and voluminous battle with a stomach virus. Then again, I recalled the axiom that visibility equals safety out on the water.

After a short flight, our pilot set the Cessna Caravan down with admirable ease and grace. Whatever apprehensions I might have harbored had fully evaporated by the time we taxied up to a weedy spit. When we had all of our gear unloaded, the plane took to the air once again and we were on our own. It was just as simple as that. Our adventure was underway.

It was an easy paddle to our island home. We had a tailwind, which was appreciated but not at all needed. Our kayaks were amazingly swift. Chris looked entirely at home on the water. He seemed to be a natural. He asked me how much kayaking I had done. I shared that I was a newcomer to the sport, that this was only my sixth time in a kayak, and that this was the first time I had ever had my new double blade paddle in the water. Then with a big Cheshire cat grin, Chris looked over to me and said, "Well, my first time in a kayak started about ten minutes ago." I had to laugh at this, and I knew the two of us were going to get along famously.

The sky was filled with thunder and bluster all night long. However, only a scant amount of rain fell. When morning came, we had an open horizon to the north, though it appeared to be raining far off in the distance. Shafts of sunlight slanted through holes in the clouds. I said aloud, "That is where God lives." This was a line from my childhood days, and I was certain it contained much truth. Chris told me at breakfast that he woke in the wee hours to the sound my tent zipper made when I rose to secure my storm flaps. That sound was most assuredly hardwired into both our psyches. It was no doubt a symptom of our both having led numerous youth groups on summer canoe trips. Despite my hearing loss, I long ago became internally tuned to this frequency. It had the power to pull me out of a full dead slumber.

Chris shared that he likes nothing better than to set up his tent in the very heart of a storm with the treetops madly thrashing about in the wind. "Ah," he cried. "I do love adversity!" A voice rang in my head telling me that the wise man stands well clear of the lightening rod. I thought, *Okay, so I am out here camping with Odysseus. He has just pissed off Poseidon big time. Sorry, Maggie. I guess I will not be home to you for another ten years.*

That we would be rained upon—and mightily so—was a dead certainty. We both had excellent rain gear, though. Until the sky started to pop or the waves grew too high, we would be fine. At his suggestion, I followed Chris quietly along a burned-over stretch of shoreline. So silent were we that we startled a cow moose and her calf. Both were bedded down near the water's edge. Mother and babe took off in a sudden explosion of legs, and I was left chuckling. The gentle stealth possible in a kayak was a wonderful way to move across the water.

It seemed inevitable that a neophyte to the sport of kayaking would undergo some rite of baptism. Perhaps it was for the best that my time came early in the game. Yes, there was that one false step that landed me in the drink right up to my eyelids. Pulling up to our lunchtime haul-out, I misjudged the stability of the rock against which I braced my paddle. Thankfully, both the water and air temperatures were still mild.

As I busied myself with the water filter topping off a couple of Nalgene bottles, Chris had his camera lens trained upon an ant scurrying away with a piece of prosciutto twice its size. Poor creature, my guess was the little fellow did not get to enjoy Italian take-out all that often.

Chris and I were both in a mood to put some miles behind us. He took one way around a large island and I another. He signaled for me to meet him on the other side. Just for the fun of it, I ratcheted up my paddling pace and flexed my muscles happily. I soon felt that with but a bit more energy and muscle mass I could get my kayak up on step and pull a water skier. What a pleasure it was to move so swiftly without the constant whine and stink of an engine.

There must have been somebody up above looking out for us. The sky became a whirl of cobalt clouds by late afternoon. We found exactly the right sort of stopping spot at precisely the right moment for stopping. As waves began to build, the blessing of a small rock shelf presented itself with just enough space for two tents. Within minutes, we had our shelters secured for the night, with guy ropes running to the kayaks we pulled way up on shore. Chris and I huddled in the vestibule of his tent to wait out a brief but fierce deluge and to discuss dinner possibilities. We decided that pizza would be the least amount of fuss. With the backpacker's oven and all the right ingredients within arm's reach, we soon had another masterfully created meal. Chris used tortillas for each bottom and top crust. The final product resembled a hot pita sandwich or a small calzone. This was truly sensational stuff. Setting and circumstances sharpened our appetites. We found ourselves safe, dry, and well blessed with a meal hot, filling, and delightfully simple. What need had we of worry?

A brief respite allowed us to wash dishes and to stow away gear for the night. All of our small food bags went into one huge waterproof Santa Claus sack until morning. There was another ominous peal of thunder. The sky was getting ready to dump another load upon us. I scurried off to my tent thankful to have a good book and a strong flashlight. Of course, I was unable to see the lake with my tent's storm flaps secured. However, what I could hear of the waves pounding the shore made me grateful we came off the water when we did.

I have always enjoyed creature comforts every bit as much as the next fellow. To truly win my heart on a paddle trip, though, give me the make-do simplicity of a humble bivouac camp. A tarp, a fire, a pot of coffee, and a convivial attitude are my only requirements. Choosing to make the best of circumstances in such a setting has brought me much joy over the years. There was nothing especially picturesque about the tiny island camp Chris and I set up on our third day together. I doubt that many paddlers passing the site would give it a second glance. Still, it is the place my memory flashes to whenever I reflect on this trip.

Each time the wind lulled for a bit, the low roar of the rapids upriver became audible. The blue tarp kept us dry. The fire had worked its way down to a fine bed of coals. Chris and I waited out the weather and talked for hours, as though we had known each other for ages. He told me of his paddle across the continent, what motivated him, what his joys were, and what caused him to struggle. I told him of my childhood in the woods of northern Minnesota, of learning to paddle, and of exploring the border lakes by canoe as a boy. Somewhere across Canada, the paths of our pasts intersected.

As we talked through the afternoon in our hastily constructed *siwash* camp, a front moved on out, taking with it all of the clouds and rain. At sunset, the sky was clear and there was no wind at all. We were both on the water as the sun sank. We fished contentedly and absorbed the beauty and stillness of this wild place. Loons began to call right at the peak of the witching hour, as if they were on cue.

As was bound to happen, packing the kayaks became a considerably less taxing chore when we were a few days into our trip. We headed into a small bay where Chris showed me a massive beaver lodge he had explored while he was out fishing the previous evening. It was actually far more than one lodge. The entire shoreline for several dozen yards was all structure modified by thousands of beaver sticks, mud, and an awful lot of time. There had to have been a couple of miles of tunnels under all of that chewed lumber. One old member of *castor canadensis* had been swimming about just off our *siwash* camp at twilight. It gave us a bit of the old stink eye while we were fishing, and it seemed eager to have us leave. There was no sign of the furry fellow in the morning. I imagined it holed up in conference with several of its brethren plotting the rodent equivalent of Grand Coolie Dam.

We entered an area our charts labeled as the North Caribou River. This was actually a chain of several small lakes connected by swifts. Some of the swifts were marked on the map. Many were not. We paid close attention to the decrease in elevation noted on the maps. With the water level up as high as it was, we found that most of the swifts were runnable. However, our touring kayaks were not built for whitewater. They did not pivot quickly enough to execute the kind of turns required for anything larger than a simple class-one rapids. Moreover, our double-bladed touring paddles were weakest at the joints connecting the halves. Just one overly enthusiastic brace or draw done to dodge a boulder could have had dire consequences. Chris and I only ran the easy stuff, and that was just fine with me. I mused that as I aged, my level of paranoia about messing up catastrophically was in good balance with my level of skill. Besides, I concluded, I had yet to come close to drowning on a portage.

Where portages did exist on this route, they were invariably covered with log skids cut to make horsing a motorboat across less of a grueling chore. That was all fine for motorboats, but meant that anyone else doing a portage was essentially running an obstacle course. We emptied the kayaks and loaded up the Santa Claus sack to portage around one rather wicked set of rapids. It was a classic island set. One chute ran down river right while the main channel was river left. A small island divided the two channels. Ledges in the left channel precluded our running this set safely, and the sharp turn in the right channel pretty much nixed that run. We found that the portage was not at all bad. Chris took the stern of both kayaks at once and I took the bows. This worked well, and afterward my arms were a good foot and a half longer than my legs.

The day grew warm. Chris and I took a short detour to find out if we could paddle into Hodgson Lake, simply to see what was there. We ran a small swift with no mishap, rounded a point, and found a huge eagle's nest. Not a day had passed without the presence of several eagles. Ospreys were in the area, also. On this morning we were blessed with quite a spectacular avian display. As if in a choreographed aerial performance, one osprey was working over a riffle near us. It spied a fish and went into a dive. This got our attention and the attention of two additional ospreys. Soon we had a wonderful feathered trio diving, circling, and snatching away fish as we watched in full amazement.

A stony rapids that poured into the North Caribou River thwarted our way into Hodgson Lake. There was no portage to be found there, so we backtracked and turned our energies downstream to explore Seeseep

Lake. There were many rock outcrops along the shore, giving the lake a rugged character. There were easily a dozen good places to set up camp along this wild shore.

Our home for the night was a pleasant island within sight of the rapids into Staunton Lake. After portaging, we were both dripping with sweat. It had to have been somewhere in the mid-eighties Fahrenheit, and there was neither a cloud nor a breath of wind to be found. Fishing became priority three. First came setting up the tents, and then came a most welcome and most cooling scrub swim.

Neither of us was particularly hungry when evening came. Heat seemed to have shattered our appetites. We downed a lot of water, fanaticized about ice cream, and prepared a simple pasta and cheese supper with some dried beef added. I paddled over to fish below the rapids after supper, but only snake jackfish were biting. Fishing off the campsite at dusk yielded more of those skinny hammer-handle jackfish and a couple of tiny walleyes. We made plans for the following afternoon to set aside time to find a sizeable keeper or two for a fish supper. I decided to keep the rain fly off my tent in order to stargaze until sleep got the better of me. My last thought before drifting off came as petition, *God, if I do my best to live an honorable life and say my prayers, may I please come back as an osprey?*

What followed was another hot gem of a day. There had been stars galore the previous night, and I even spotted a faint hint of the *aurora borealis*. I was starting to notice some alarming difficulty in tying fishing knots. Perhaps this was yet another reminder that I was most certainly getting older. The fine motor dexterity with my right hand had become pathetic. As I reclined in my sleeping bag to wait for the stars to appear, I practiced a little sign language. I ran through the manual alphabet left-handed from A to Z and back again. No problem. Then I tried to do the same with my right hand. Whoa! I found no strength or flexibility there at all. My digits had all turned to mashed potatoes. Perhaps I had pinched a nerve. Maybe it was simply tendonitis. Fortunately, it did not really hurt and my paddling was not affected.

We were graced with a lovely morning for playing on the river. We paddled through the standing waves at the end of several swifts and thoroughly enjoyed the sloshy bounce. Chris referred to this action as riding on out on the gravy train. After scouting and running one beautiful chute, we hauled out and fixed lunch. I was not at all certain just what the winds aloft were up to, but the air currents created a magnificent *williwaw* right across the river from us. If you were watching television in the late 1960s, perhaps you recall the commercials for Ajax, which cleans like a white tornado. This wind dance was just like that ad. It lasted several seconds, adding a bit more magic to an already enchanted spot.

Perhaps we were simply getting cocky. Pushing our luck by a considerable measure, we fully indulged in the joy of the day and ran the risk of having the pleasures of the river literally wash over us. Chris and I took one of the final runs of the trip straight down the gravy train side by side, just to show off for the ducks. This was a kick. Out came the fishing rods. It was walleye supper or bust.

Well, it looked like it would be bust for some while there. We went to shore near Agutua Portage and made a simple camp. The rapids into the lake were certainly runnable, but they were considerably rough. Why tempt fate overly much and put a sour close on an excellent trip? While I was casting from shore near our campsite, Chris took his fishing equipment back upriver to work a few pools. There was not much action for either of us in the heat of the afternoon. A couple of quiet hours passed. Finally, Chris let out a great whoop. He had caught our meal. When he paddled in toward camp, he tossed the fish up to shore. It was a fine walleye, and it landed squarely on the seat of my kayak.

While the two of us leisurely indulged in preparing supper, a motorboat with four folks we figured were probably locals made a run up the rapids and then back down again. There were two or three cabins just across the lake from the far end of the portage. I had noticed earlier that two boats were anchored immediately below the rapids with about a half dozen people fishing. I did not, however, notice much catching occurring. I was curious just what these Anishinaabe thought of our kayaks or of us, assuming they gave us something more than a passing glance.

Just before dark, a man and a woman walked into our camp. Soon another fellow, quite a bit younger, followed them. All three were Anishinaabe and considerably less than loquacious. This trio left their boat at the end of the rapids and walked along the riverbank to where Chris and I were sitting around our campfire. After seeing no one for the past few days, we were now being gawked at mightily and were clearly the center of attention. Doubtless we were the center of much unvoiced curiosity. This felt odd and more than a little uncomfortable. Only the older fellow spoke. He did not say much, but Chris and I both sensed that our boats intrigued him. He finally asked where we had come from and how far we had traveled. He then voiced some concern about our campfire, but I felt pretty certain he did this just to have something more to say. We assured him—or at least tried to—that he had no cause to worry. Our fire would be properly extinguished.

When all three had taken their leave of us, it finally crashed in on me that I could stand to be a good deal more hospitable. Coffee would have been easy enough to rustle up and share. We should have at least made the offer. Unbidden they may have been; these folks still deserved cordiality and welcome. There was a lesson in this, and I stowed it away for next time.

The moon that night was close to being full. The sky at sundown told us that clouds would obscure the moon some, but I was determined to keep my tent flaps rolled back to watch for it. Our fish supper had been an excellent feed in spite of our discovering we had forgotten a certain half bottle of Chianti set against a tree at our first campsite. Perhaps the moon was the cause of my restlessness. Nothing whatsoever was troubling me, but sleep just did not come easily. As I sat in my tent with my sleeping bag wrapped about me, I listened to the rapids. I remembered a game I used to play as a boy. In this game I would think of a voice that I knew well singing a familiar song. Then I would try to listen for snatches of that song in the roar of the rapids. I had known since my boyhood days that there were playful spirits living in all moving waters. Here, then, were my songs for kayaking. I listened to this music well into the wee hours with my soul as contented as it had ever been.

I pulled my watch from the bottom of a stuff sack and saw that it was just a bit after three in the morning. I had long since given up on getting any sleep. A delicate patter of light drizzle was hitting my tent fly. I dug out my rain gear, suited up, and quietly walked across the portage. Muffled snoring coming from the other tent as I passed assured me that I had not disturbed Chris. The sound of the rapids would likely have drowned out that of my tent zipper even if Chris had been awake. The portage ran perpendicular to the rapids and ended in a small cove. I watched the lake for quite a while, delighted to see the drizzle fade and then disappear altogether. I turned, and halfway across the portage I stopped to sit under a spruce tree on a clump of moss. There was no moodiness or sadness in me. There was only the stillness, and this stillness set me to pondering. I thought about how there is often this same awkward time in most adventures. It comes near the end when it is a little too late for action and a bit too soon for memories. I said a simple prayer of thanksgiving and returned to my tent.

After daybreak, Chris and I packed up camp and made our way across the final portage of our trip. We then paddled out of the cove and around to the base of the rapids to fish for a while in the current. None of the locals we encountered the previous evening had yet ventured out, save for about a half-dozen noisy terns. I discovered a looser grip on my paddle helped to lessen the trouble I was having with dexterity. After paddling a mile or more down the lake, we hauled out at a little island. Here we got a simple breakfast going and set the tents out to dry a bit before repacking them.

The heat of the morning set in before long, and we started to paddle down Agutua Arm looking for an easy spot to hook up with our scheduled floatplane. Most of the shoreline we passed was rocky. The shoals and protruding boulders precluded working a plane in close to shore. Dinging up a float would not be a good way to end a great trip. As it turned out, our pilot flew directly over us just as we rounded a small island. He was flying Bernie's de Havilland Single Otter and could not see us at all. Chris used a small hand-held radio to guide the pilot to us, and we loaded up right out on the lake. This became a bit of a balancing act, but the three of us worked together. We managed to not drop any gear or anybody overboard. The rudder assembly of my kayak had to be removed, as there was a chance it would interfere with the floats. We staggered the two boats and they rode on the same side. In retrospect, loading my kayak stern first probably would have kept the rudder clear, but the last thing I wanted to do at the time was second-guess an experienced bush pilot. Confession has always been a balm for the soul. Clumsy me. I came within a fraction of an inch of knocking the entire kayak rudder assembly out the door and into the drink as I stepped up into the plane.

The flight back to the airfield at Pickle Lake took us a little over an hour. Chris had just one day to prepare before heading out again on another trip. Ever imperturbable, the fact that a deadline would be looming did not appear to faze him in the slightest. He was bound for the Otoskwin River on a guiding gig with a family of canoe trippers. I had two days of fly-fishing for brook trout ahead of me on a tributary of the Albany River. Then it would be time to head home to Maggie, a sunny deck, and a fine glass of wine.

After this initial kayak trip, I was certain that there would be many more such excursions in my future. The key lessons from that long-ago journey were simple, and they still echo. One blade or two, it matters infinitely more that you paddle than how you paddle. Be ever grateful for any time spent in the good woods. Just as you would engage a solid brace heading into the gravy train, lean your weight upon what you love best. It will keep you upright.

Imagining Michipicoten

WHAT DOES THE shape of Lake Superior remind you of when you look at a map? Some people see the head of a wolf. I have always imagined it to be the elongated head of a greyhound. Granted, this is one weirdly abstract beast with a rather pronounced deformity around its muzzle somewhere between Duluth and the community of Bayfield, Wisconsin. Imagine that the Keweenaw Peninsula is in the area of the hound's mouth. Whitefish Point and Batchawana Bay are opposite sides of its collar. Stick with this image for a moment and picture where the beast's ear would be. If Isle Royale constitutes this hound's eye, a second large island tucked up in the northeast part of the lake makes up the left ear. This is Michipicoten Island.

Michipicoten Island, the third-largest island on Lake Superior, is just about as remote a spot as you are apt to find on this huge lake. It is richly steeped in both history and legend. The Anishinaabe were by ancient tradition leery of the island and avoided it as a bad spirit place. Part of its mystique comes from optical illusions commonly experienced when gazing out at it from the mainland. The island appears to be transforming itself constantly. In certain light conditions, it appears to float above the horizon line. Sometimes there appears to be a flattening at its top despite its rugged topography. Michipicoten Island can be seen as having shifted to the left or to the right of where you saw it just a short while earlier. Other times it is not visible at all. Bring to it a reverent spirit and a keen sense of curiosity, and you may likewise find yourself transformed.

If impermanence has led to the mystique of Michipicoten Island, so, too, has circumstance. Anishinaabe stories tell of hunting parties visiting the island and never returning. Ill fate typically befell any tribesmen who would canoe to Michipicoten to gather from its abundance of copper nuggets. Illness, starvation, or other grave misfortune would hit the paddlers and their family members upon their return to mainland encampments.

By the late nineteenth century, prospectors were extracting from Michipicoten Island far more than just a canoe load of the island's copper nuggets. In the years just prior to the American Civil War, mines in Michigan's Keweenaw Peninsula were beginning to boom. Optimistic speculators turned their attention to the north shore of Lake Superior and to Michipicoten Island, reasoning that these regions shared a similar geological makeup to northern Michigan and would yield similar mineral wealth. The northwest corner of Michipicoten Island seemed the most promising, and it was there that the principal investors of the Quebec and Lake Superior Mining Association pinned their strongest hopes.

Tramp about the ruins of the old Quebec Mine. Allow your imagination to have free rein, and you will be amazed at what must have occurred here. If there is but the slightest bit of sympathy anywhere in your heart, you will truly feel for the plight of the hapless Cornish, Irish, and French-Canadian miners stationed here in what must have seemed like the edge of the known world. In the age of steam power and muscle, deep mine shafts were sunk and in constant need of being pumped dry. The deepest shaft went down more than 500 feet. Four huge boilers were set up to power a stamping mill. Some 150 to 200 workers were employed here at the height of the mine's activity in the 1880s. Strewn over an area of a bit less than a square mile are the remnants of stone buildings, a sawmill, a small farm, and enough outsized iron wheels, flanges, and rails to build an Erector Set for Paul Bunyan.

Now the island has no permanent residents, and much of it is conserved as an Ontario provincial park. Even the lighthouses around the island are unpeopled, having been automated quite some time ago. Silence has returned to the northwest corner of Michipicoten. Moss, spruce, and balsam firs now blanket the site that once held so much activity. Whiskey bottles and old condiment jars still poke through the duff and soil in plentitude. Tomorrow even these will be covered. Michipicoten Island will eventually reclaim her own.

In July of 2004, Peter Van Wyk, Glen Bowers, and I teamed up to explore Michipicoten Island by kayak. The trio of us ventured out to the island aboard an old fishing tug captained by a crusty, tough-as-guts commercial fisherman named Horst Anderson. A small brass plaque outside the steering house of his tug read: THIS IS MY SHIP AND I'LL DO AS I DAMN PLEASE! Kurt, Horst's son and fishing partner, stood grinning. He and I both gazed out from the stern watching the boat's wake. At one point there was a significant jag in the wake, followed by the evidence of an abrupt correction. Chuckling, Kurt shared, "The old man must have dozed off a bit there."

In addition to nets, ice, and fish boxes, the cargo that July morning included a trio of kayaks, each as stuffed with gear as a cocktail olive is stuffed with pimento. I never took the chance to ask Horst his opinion regarding kayaks and the people who venture to his part of the big lake for recreation. I figured it was best not to rile the fellow who is your ticket back to the mainland. Horst seemed an easy person to rile. Were we to him anything more than freight that talks? The more cantankerous boat owners I have encountered while paddling on Lake Superior tended to refer to us kayakers as mere flotsam in their path to the next dock. Perhaps Horst was truly grateful that Peter, Glen, and I were more animated than his usual cargo of newly iced lake trout, but you could never decipher that from his gruff countenance.

Our crossing went well, as the lake was delightfully calm. We pulled into Cozens Cove shortly before noon. Why take a tug? The distance from the mainland to this pleasant cove is substantial, with more than twenty miles wide open to winds. A fellow could spend a good

long while on shore waiting for ideal paddling conditions only to have the wind and waves kick up and
knock him flat once started. The boat ride was a concession to safety and to time constraints. Besides, it
was grand to see the Pukaskwa Coast fade in the distance. We had the pleasure of watching the coast from
various vantage points on Michipicoten's north shore
during our week-long circumnavigation of the island.
The rugged Pukaskwa headlands appeared to flatten,
fade, expand, and change configuration in a reverse
position of the mirage phenomenon that first attracted
me to Michipicoten Island. Like a Canadian version of
Brigadoon, sky and water and light all collaborated to
toy with my head.

A geologist would find this island a slice of paradise
and could explain both its volcanic origin and its mineral composition. Our trio of kayakers had no geologist, but each of us found his own interpretation of
what is heavenly. My paddling companions and I were
all strangers to one another the day before our crossing. Glen was an electrical engineer from Plymouth,
Michigan. Peter split his time between guiding kayak
trips for an outfitting firm based in Wawa, Ontario, and
working for a resort on Lake Huron. We each looked
down through the cold clearness underneath our
kayaks and traced the veins of white quartz that extended from the dark rocks on the shore. These veins
crisscrossed all over. The transparency of the water was
mesmerizing, particularly when coupled with the exten-
sion and patterning of the quartz veins. All of this might

easily have snared us into believing that the water was not even there. A slight tip to the left or to the right would have quickly put an end to that notion.

It would not be difficult to measure the distance the three of us paddled together during our exploration of Michipicoten Island. For me, though, a fine journey has little to do with the accumulation of miles. The more completely I forget what day it is, the larger the grin on my face. I undergo a transformation after a few days traveling by kayak and find myself becoming a more contented and less complicated being. My goal when paddling is to take joy from living in and living for each moment. More often than not I find those moments to be thoroughly life-giving. In that respect, I have been abundantly blessed.

Rockhopping along the shore with a mug of hot coffee in one hand may be as close to dancing as I will ever come. This has become something of a morning ritual for me on paddle trips. I usually do not go far— just far enough to see what is around the next point. I try not to make too much noise. Michipicoten mornings usually included loons off shore. One morning, I watched a woodland caribou feeding within inches of Glen's tent. On another morning, I watched a fox stretch, scratch, and give a gaping yawn just moments after I had done exactly the same.

As Glen, Peter, and I hiked along the shoreline or paddled close to the sea caves on Michipicoten's north side, we seemed to be forever startling beavers. These pugnacious fur balls exist on the island in such profusion and are so active that you would be wise to pitch your tent well away from any deciduous trees. One beaver came careening down the rocks and missed Glen's foot by mere inches on its mad scramble to the lake. From the safety of the water, it turned to face us and hissed its displeasure. I spooked another as badly as it spooked me when I swung the bow of my kayak into a dark niche only to have that large stone in the far back jump up and head for the water.

An otter or an owl might try to take a small beaver kit. The adults, on the other hand, really have no natural predator on the island. There are no bears on Michipicoten. As the island is a provincial park, beaver are not trapped. Folks stopped turning them into hats years ago. I imagine that out on the island these creatures have become complacent, maybe even a bit smug, sensing their own impunity. The odd hiker or transient paddler then happens by and frightens the stuffing out of them.

Two sandhill cranes were feeding in the little creek just to the east of where we stopped for a stretch break one afternoon. What little noise we made must have been enough to make them uneasy about lingering. They flew right over us, calling as they went. I love the preposterous size of cranes and their gravelly cackle. If Tom Waits had been born a bird, he would surely have been a sandhill crane.

We found a great deal to explore on and around Michipicoten. Torso rotation, which is a part of proper paddling technique, was a given as we gazed about scanning the shoreline. It was almost as if our heads were on turrets, so eager were we to take in all there was to see. When ashore one morning, we noticed how a creek bed had been sculpted to form the perfect bathtub at the base of a small cataract. Each of us found agates and also bits of sea glass that glinted in the sun, catching the eye. Peter led us up into the massive sea cave that was once used by the Quebec Mine as a storage site for blasting powder. I hesitated at its entrance, imaging the enormity of whatever beaver might lurk in its vast recesses.

You are likely aware of the American writer Alice Walker and of her affinity for shades of purple. As I paddled, I wondered if she had ever seen harebells in July set against the dark wet rocks of a Lake Superior island. These cheerful little beauties (*Campanula rotundifolia*) were all over the south side of Green Island, which is just off the southwest end of Michipicoten. I trust they would uplift anyone's sagging spirit. Lichens grew thick on many of the rocks. Inland on Green Island, our home for one night, the sphagnum moss was more than a foot thick in places, forming a dense carpet for the forest floor. The forest there was the same impenetrable spruce jungle found on Michipicoten. No one could ever move through this stuff in a hurry.

Peter and I took a night paddle around Green Island. Glen stayed in camp tending the fire. I can see him yet in my mind's eye. I see only his silhouette. I remember how Peter and I needed a few moments to allow our eyes to adjust to the darkness before making our wordless circumnavigation. The moon was just two nights away from being full. The stars astounded us and seemed almost approachable. In the stillness, I took care to make my paddling as quiet as my breathing. It was a magic, bewitching time. A few faint fingers of the *aurora* played overhead. We paddled around the island twice in silence. The lake and the sky became one, and I felt as if I might gently melt away into the shimmer of moonlight on the water.

In addition to Glen's silhouette, a second image comes into my head when I think of him. He is a fellow of great creative energy. Do you remember the cartoon character Gyro Gearloose from the old Walt Disney comics? He was the quintessential single-minded inventor of all manner of contraptions needed or otherwise. I cannot imagine Glen for long without thinking of this character. I do mean that as a sincere complement. Save for Fred Rogers, just about all of my heroes are cartoons. You could almost hear Glen's mind at work when he was engaged in problem solving. I kept looking for that little lightbulb above his head to come on, because I knew it had to be there somewhere.

When the lithium power cell on his camera puked out midtrip, Glen got busy. He first gathered duct tape, two AA batteries from a flashlight, and pair of wire-cored twist ties from bread bags. He then tapped into the camera contacts and got the sucker running like a champ. At the beginning of our excursion, Glen set a quota of a roll of film per day for himself. This little battery glitch did not slow him down at all. I admire such creative tenacity.

As we walked up the path from the shore of Davieaux Island to the lighthouse, Peter commented that he would give his eyeteeth to live in this quiet place. We both tried to envision what walking this same path every day would be like for anyone who made this island his home. How much more would such a person notice that we did not, for the simple act of slowing his pace and not being transient? Peter made a similar comment when we ate lunch near a tiny cabin in Cozens Cove. The cabin was of fairly recent construction, with a metal roof and a nice front window facing the water. "This is all I would need," he shared.

Peter is just a tad more than half my age. He has worked in several of the true jewel spots of Canada leading hiking and paddle trips. I chuckle when I remember his descriptions of the raft trips he has guided and the culinary focus they had. He called those excursions float and bloat trips. Peter is exceptionally skilled at his craft. Glen and I both felt fortunate to have him as the guide on our exploration of Michipicoten Island. The urge to go play in the woods is strong in him. It is strong in me as well, but I will never again have his level of energy. I did sense a bit of angst in Peter regarding his desire to put down roots. Perhaps this was entirely a misread on my part. Still, I could not help but feel that he and I were looking for the same kernel of peace but from opposite ends of the age continuum. I wish him well on his journey.

When I imagine Michipicoten Island, it is the image of our camp at East Sand Bay that most readily rushes to my mind. I can easily picture the obsidian and cobalt hues of the water and the fierce curling of the waves as we paddled past Dixon Reef just before making camp. I picture Glen walking the long beach, finding a coho salmon washed up on the rocks, and building an elaborate bridge for himself across the little creek near his tent site as only a true engineer would. I can picture Peter unloading his kayak and heading out again to paddle and play in the surf. He lost his favorite hat, but he kept his smile. I can even see myself clearly through the lens of my memory. I am that stubborn little cuss standing in the pouring rain with a mound of birchbark four times the size of his head and a pack of matches. It sure took a lot of persistence to get that fire going, but what a blaze it became. I know in my child's heart that fire is never going to die.

Old Man's River

A LL TOO OFTEN, paddle trips are of necessity tightly scheduled affairs set to run in the push and pain mode as opposed to being geared simply for putzing and play. If only we had the time to linger in paradise doing what most brings about a contented heart. All too often, fishing becomes merely a sidebar activity on a paddle trip, with too few hours available to explore the plunge pools and honey holes. If only we could stop and fish where the angling looks most promising without the slightest concern for making miles or meeting a deadline.

My wife blessed me with the gift of a fly-fishing trip on the Sutton River in July of 2005, the summer I turned fifty. I joined Tom and Big Mike for a week of just the sort of angling that burrows into a fellow's dreams and makes him awaken with a smile that lasts all morning. One advantage of crossing the threshold into geezerhood is the ease with which you can allow yourself to become totally spoiled without feeling all that guilty about it. Entitlement, whether justified or otherwise, has suddenly become something you can talk yourself into without too great a struggle. The gray around your temples says you better take care of your joys while you still can. For seven glorious days, we were spoiled rotten. We had all the brook trout fishing we could handle in a rare bit of paradise where the fish were in amazing abundance.

The little town of Pickle Lake, Ontario, was once again our jumping-off place. It is literally at the end of the line. Highway 599 was built as a haul road decades ago to service a couple of gold mines. The mines are entirely played out now, but a few adventurous and enterprising souls have set up shop here in order to provide paddlers and fisher folk access to another type of gold. A two-hour ride by floatplane from Pickle Lake gets you into Hawley Lake and the headwaters of the Sutton River. This river flows some eighty-five miles before emptying into Hudson Bay near Cape Henrietta Maria, just north of the fifty-fifth parallel.

It is a long way from anywhere to Xavier Chookomoolin's fish camp on Hawley Lake. Here you will find a small handful of one-room cabins and outbuildings fashioned from black spruce logs. There is a central building with a kitchen and a dining area. It is all quite rustic and a bit snug, but the camp is clean and comfortable. If you expect Cub Med, you are on the wrong river.

Hawley Lake and the Sutton River itself are both geological oddities. In a land ribboned with tannic streams and pocked with muskeg ponds, Hawley Lake and the river that drains it have limestone bedrock and are gin-clear. If I were a trout, I would be perfectly content living there. The water in the Sutton River is of the proper temperature and PH balance to provide just the sort of habitat in which large brook trout thrive, and thrive they do. There is a good pebble bottom on much of the river, serving as excellent material for spawning redds. There are water insects in sufficient numbers to provide abundant feed. However, these brookies travel out to Hudson Bay to bulk up prior to spawning.

Do not be misled. The sea run and spawning cycle these brook trout undergo may make you think of salmon. Indeed, some of these fish come near salmon in size, averaging better than three pounds and around twenty-two inches. Sutton River brookies do not head upstream, spawn once, and then die. The trout we caught—and there were a good many—make an annual feeding trip to Hudson Bay and are back in the river weeks before spawning. Salt water turns down the hues in the skin of these fish. The longer these trout are back in fresh water, the brighter their colorization becomes. We were not casting our flies to dying fish. These brookies are filled with the beauty and vigor of life.

There were five of us traveling and fishing together. In this group of friends, I was the second youngest by only a few months. None of us could claim to be a little boy any longer, except at heart, of course. The other four were all men of the business world and highly skilled at what they did for a living. I had chosen to make my livelihood as an educator. Part of what each of the five of us did to make a life was to go fly-fishing. Each of us possessed a definite passion for the sport, and mine had begun to border on sweet obsession.

The logistics of a fishing trip like this one could be a bit daunting. We were blessed to have the assistance of Lynn and Bernie Cox of North Star Air and Canoe Frontiers Outfitting. Masterful attention to detail and consistent top-drawer service, all given with a good sense of humor, helped these folks build a reputation as the best in the bush. We had glitch-free flights, ate like kings, slept comfortably, and fished each day until our arms ached. It was a slice of heaven.

Xavier Chookomoolin's Cree family has lived in the area of Hawley Lake for several generations. He worked diligently to get us down the river to our tent camp and to put us on fish each day at various pools downstream from our camp. Lynn and Bernie handled all of the other logistics. They even sent us out with our own cook to look after us. This was Jerry Nichols, a young special education teacher from Thunder Bay. Xavier's river savvy and Canoe Frontier's attention to detail made an unbeatable combination, allowing the five of us to become thoroughly spoiled and to focus solely on fly-fishing.

Spending a week on the Sutton River helped me hone my skill set as a fly angler. The river was wide enough and shallow enough to allow a person to stand or wade just about anywhere and to cast a fly without having to worry about snagging a willow bush on the backcast. Sight casting to large trout was possible and a fully engaging challenge. The brookies were in such plenitude that we could not help but become more adept at setting a hook, playing a fish, and releasing a catch quickly. Though I still do not cast with any great amount of finesse, I found that I could usually get the bug to the fish and link up in a not-too-shabby manner. Being among four charitable friends not centered on competing with one another was a huge plus. We all shared gear, advice, and good-natured ribbing with ease. If there was a harsh word from one person to another spoken all week, I sure did not hear it.

One thing I did hear repeatedly was Big Mike's infectious, full-bodied laugh. He let loose each time he hooked into a trout, and he hooked a good many. Big Mike would always signal his first catch of each day with an irrepressible, echoing guffaw, followed by his signature expression, "I'm on the board!"

Tom has long been the type of skilled, patient fly angler I still aspire to become. He is a good ten inches taller than I am, and perhaps his success on the Sutton was in part attributable to being able to wade deeper due to his height. Tom was also generous with his flare for cooking fish. We released all of our trout save for two fine brookies, which Tom expertly prepared over a bed of coals and served as hors d'oeuvrs one evening. He and Big Mike were college roommates and have been the best of friends ever since.

Each of us was fully aware of the richness and rarity of our shared journey, and we grew giddy catching large fish. Connecting with one of those strong, healthy, wild trout was a lot like setting off an explosive charge. Your whole body would tense up with anticipation and then *boom!* The anfractuous dance began.

We did not use nets, as we decided they were too hard on the fish. Sutton River trout were fighters, and it could sometimes take a while to bring a hooked beauty to hand. The barbless fly would be quickly removed, ideally with the trout still in the water. It was sometimes necessary to spend several minutes reviving a fish. This we did with equal parts respect and gratitude. It was while taking measures to help spent trout recover that we each had the opportunity to examine the impossibly complex jumble of swirls and dots with halos that make up the skin of a wild brookie. Each trout was a marvelous gift to behold.

Jerry Nichols worked hard to make ours a comfortable camp. He proved to be an excellent cook. Lynn and Bernie had supplied him with enough bread, fresh meat, vegetables, and libation to run a restaurant for a month. Much of the food was on ice, and the weather was such that the ice lasted our entire week. Food did not spoil. Our tent camp was several miles down the river from Hawley Lake and set up near some mighty fine fishing water. Jerry brought along a considerable amount of gear, as ours was the first of five groups booked to use the tented camp during the peak season. He had with him the largest tarp I have ever seen. The thing could have covered an aircraft carrier. We doubled it over a simple log pole structure to make an excellent sheltered kitchen area. We also set up two large tents, complete with cots and pads for sleeping bags. Compared with most of our paddle trip experiences, we were living pretty posh. Each of us had a camp chair to pull up to the fire. After a good day of fishing, there was considerable drink, lively conversation, and a cheerful blaze. Often the night sky was clear enough to stargaze. Indeed, we had our own planetarium. Twice we had spectacular displays of northern lights.

That persistent ringing in my ears was not a symptom of presbycusis. It was the result of several hours spent in Xavier's freighter canoe with its noisy eight-horse kicker. The bump-and-go procedures necessary to get through the shallows and around the rock gardens could take a toll on a fellow's spine. Xavier was an amazing fellow to watch as he negotiated an upstream run through a swift. Balance, timing, and positioning were of greater importance in this process than simple brute force, though there was plenty of that, too. When nothing else worked, we all piled out of the craft and pushed. One nasty spot on a downstream run completely sheared off the lower unit of Xavier's motor. The break was a long time coming. He had used the kicker for about ten years. Fortunately, we had a spare for the Zodiac raft we brought along with us. After putting us on fish and returning us to our tent camp, Xavier made the long slog back to Hawley Lake. There he rebuilt his eight-horse with spare parts before linking up with us the next morning.

In my favorite mental image of Xavier Chookomoolin, he is seated in a camp chair at the end of a long day. In his left hand he has a fine cigar going that one of the fellows just gave him. In his right hand is a mug of grog Jerry supplied as he pulled his chair up to the fire. He smiles at us and says, "I am the only guide in the north woods you pay to look after."

There was a fine little pool one hundred yards or so upstream from the tent camp. I came across this spot the first day on the river after we got everything situated. After morning coffee but before breakfast, I routinely put on my waders and went to this pool to catch my first trout of the day. It became a fine ritual, and I found myself wishing I could start more of my days in the same manner. I chuckle when I think of Jerry. He had a similar thing going near the start of our trip with his spinning rod. One morning he caught and released five brookies before the coffee had perked. Jerry brought along a new fly rod and reel, but he had never been fly-fishing before. "Iron men" was what Xavier called spin casters who chuck Mepps spinners and Blue Fox spoons at Sutton River trout. "Pencil dicks" was Jerry's pejorative for fly anglers with nine-foot rods. It was thus that our small group became known as Pencil Dicks in Paradise.

To his credit, Jerry learned to use his new fly rod, and he could throw a pretty good cast by the end of our trip. We gave him a few pointers, some bugs, and tippet material. We ribbed him a bit about having his fly line spooled upside-down and backwards. He was probably still an iron man at heart, but I admired his enthusiasm and his willingness to learn something new.

Most of us had previously witnessed the way spin tackle with treble hooks could devastate a trout. Since catch-and-release fishing had long been the standard on the Sutton, iron men were always encouraged to clip two hooks off each spinner and pinch back the barb on the remainder. That seemed fair enough. The manner in which an angler went after a trout mattered little to me so long as water, fish, and fellow anglers were all respected. However, having crested into my fiftieth year, I decided that if I could not catch these beautiful creatures on a fly rod, I would just as soon leave them alone.

The Sutton River flows through an area transitioning from boreal forest to tundra. Our tent camp and the parts of the river we fished and explored were all in the sub-tundra zone. Black spruce and tamaracks lined the riverbanks. The forest floor was covered in a thick carpet of moss and lichen. Stunted blueberry bushes were abundant and full, and we found it odd that the berries were actually oblong. Seeing this forest from the air made me think of a couple of lines from the Robert Service poem "Spell of the Yukon": "Some say God was tired when He made it; Some say it's a fine land to shun . . ." Perhaps the area lacked the drop-dead beauty of the Canadian Shield country. Still, this was where the trout lived. I found the place kind of grows on a person after a while.

Caribou seemed to like the area. Our group spotted two, the second of which Xavier stopped in its tracks with a high-pitched whistle. We saw bald eagles and a few ospreys. They likely fed pretty well on fish. Our week on the Sutton River did not include a trip out to

Hudson Bay. Therefore, we did not encounter any of the many polar bears that summer in the area between the mouth of the Sutton and the mouth of the Winisk River to the northwest. That was an experience for another time, perhaps. I figured the whiskey jacks must all have internal dinner bells. They never failed to be around at meal times. Jerry placed a small bowl of food scraps out for them near his kitchen.

When the time came for reflection, there was much I could claim to have gained from my first half-century. I had learned how to be satisfied with enough. I did not need to catch the most trout or the largest trout to be happy as a fly angler. Fly-fishing was never my idea of a blood sport, and I always fished much better whenever I left my ego at home. Xavier caught me with a huge smile on my face as I piled out of his freighter canoe one evening and asked if I had a contented heart. Yes, I most assuredly did. I was also given ample opportunity to learn humility. I backed off a rock and went in over my wader tops on our final afternoon of angling just as the others were hot into the fish. It was a long, cold ride back to camp. I had learned when not to speak or make a sarcastic remark. Admittedly, there was still room for improvement. More often than ever before, I found myself asking, "Will this loaded comment really benefit anyone?" I had learned the value of good friends by losing a few. I had learned some measure of patience. A voice inside said to always take the time to undo a wind knot from your line. The trout can wait. If you do not end up catching it, then it simply was not yours to catch.

The most important lessons in my life all have to do with gratitude and trust. When you share a dream trip with a small group of friends, your dream is in their hands and their dreams are in yours. I trust that the good woods will always offer what I most need when it is once again time for me to pinch back the barbs on a negative attitude. For that I am truly grateful.

There were several little nicks and cuts on my hands and fingers when I returned home from the Sutton River. These were from sharp hooks, tight lines, and trout teeth. They all healed and cleared up in time. The Sutton River itself has nicked my heart, though, and that is bound to last. As I take my chair at the campfire, I am grateful that I possess a contented heart and am well pleased with the type of old man I am becoming.

The Company You Keep

CABIN FEVER AND a severe midwinter itch to go paddling prompted my call to a trusted outfitter. Parking my agenda, I agreed to the outfitter's suggestion
and signed on to become a tag-along member for a
July trip to Lake Superior's Pukaskwa Coast. I gave full
control to serendipity and came up aces.

The Canadian shore of Lake Superior is a freshwater paddler's paradise, and Ontario's Pukaskwa National Park is for any kayaker the true jewel in the
crown. Pukaskwa (pronounced puck-uh-saw) comes
from an Anishinaabe term depicting the action of extracting marrow from cooked animal bones. That may
not conjure the loveliest of images. Despite the nomen-
clature, the rugged, elemental features of this coastline
touch a responding chord in my soul, and I return here
for spiritual renewal. I find in the roots of the gnarled
cedar trees clinging to rocks, growing where no root
growth or nourishment seems possible, testimonies of
faith and endurance. I find hope and courage in the
tiny harebells, with their splash of purple offsetting the
dark grays of granite and basalt ledge rock.

Paul and Sally Harris shared their 2008 paddle trip
with me. We had never met, but a terrific rapport was

budding well before we got the boats in the water. This unique couple spends part of each year teaching at Tumaini University in Iringa, Tanzania. Sally is an English professor. Shortly before our paddle trip, she had been awarded a Fulbright Scholar Grant. She would spend much of the upcoming school year in Tanzania teaching legal writing. Paul is an assistant pastor of a Lutheran church in Eagan, Minnesota. When in Tanzania, he teaches church history and theology classes at Tumaini. He is also involved as an advisor to programs in Tanzania designed to spur development and ease the plight of the impoverished. Rarely have I ever encountered such an energetic, enthusiastic, and committed couple. The two celebrated their forty-first wedding anniversary while we paddled together.

James Roberts was the outfitter's choice as guide for our ten-day paddle trip. He is a skilled and accomplished surf kayaker with a great sense of humor and a strong love for the Canadian wild. James grew up on the Isle of Wight. He moved to Canada about five years prior to our trip together, and now makes his home in Parry Sound, Ontario, where he and his wife run the Ontario Sea Kayak Centre.

Our tiny flotilla was every bit as varied as the people who propelled it. James paddled a Greenland-style kayak, made in Canada by Boreal Designs. It was a top of the range Ellesmere model, quite sleek and fast. I paddled my beloved P and H Capella, made in England. I have no idea what the P or the H stand for, but I suspect it might be "purity and harmony." On a bad day, that might become "piss and hassle." This boat and I have yet to have a bad day together.

Paul and Sally built their kayak with the help of family members. It is truly a beautiful boat. The components came from a company in Annapolis, Maryland, called Chesapeake Light Craft. It is a tandem kayak made of wood with a coating of fiberglass. Yes, we did have to baby it a bit, but this was never a problem and never more than any good boat deserves. One fellow we met camped at Fish Cove summed it up well when he quipped: "It must be like paddling with a grand piano."

Whatever people's original intentions may have been, our ten-day excursion quickly shifted out of the "manic muscle" mode and into the "measure moments, not miles" mindset. The tandem moved a little slower than expected. This was especially true in the prevailing headwinds. We decided as a group to do a loop route rather than a dash from Heron Bay to Michipicoten Harbor. The slower tempo seemed to bring out the best in each of us. One delightful consequence was our having the time to explore the Pukaskwa Coast in far greater depth than any of us originally anticipated.

Over the past several summers, I had grown increasingly fond of taking my fly rod and hiking up the small feeder streams flowing into Lake Superior. Whenever I am in Pukaskwa, hiking and fly-fishing seem to meld into one single passion. On this particular trip, I found several pools and freshets along the Swallow

River, the North Swallow River, and the White Gravel River, where beauty was in abundance even though fish were not plentiful. I caught only a few small brook trout. They were all fine, healthy fish, though, and great fun to catch. It is now difficult for me to paddle past the mouth of any stream without giving into the impulse to find out what secrets exist up around the first couple of bends. It is my fervent desire to be out on Superior paddling and along its shores fishing, hiking, and exploring well into my twilight years.

Pukaskwa in July is a haven for birdlife. Bald eagles are often spotted soaring overhead or going after fish with results far more successful than my own. Peregrine falcons nest in the headlands. As we paddled from point to point past the entrance to Oiseau Bay, James and I were buzzed and startled by a hummingbird. The poor creature may have been a bit confused so far offshore. We could only speculate it had mistaken James's red kayak for some hugely outsized geranium and my yellow boat for the granddaddy of all marigolds. I love irony. *Oiseau* is the French word for "bird."

James tried to catch the weather forecast on his portable marine radio each morning and evening. The Pukaskwa Coast is about as remote a place as you can find anywhere in the Great Lakes Region. Capturing a clear radio signal in an area so punctuated with headlands, ridges, and deep valleys is not always possible. James was mighty persistent in spite of the less-than-helpful suggestions we gave him from our seats around the campfire. As he struggled with this one evening, the rest of us freely offered unsolicited advice. He could wrap his entire body in Paul's Mylar space blanket and place a slice of rudder cable from his kayak between his teeth for better reception. I suggested placing a colander or a tin funnel on his head and turning himself into an English antenna so we could all listen to the evening broadcast of the BBC World Service. With a wink to my fellow baby boomers, I added he would look just like Tom Terrific, the cartoon character from *Captain Kangaroo*. This sparked a totally unexpected response from Sally; she began to sing the *Tom Terrific* theme song with unbridled enthusiasm. I am not certain what Sally had to go through to win her Fulbright Grant. However, I do feel academia could use a bit more levity. Imagine if the process included standing on a stage somewhere and belting out two verses of the *Tom Terrific* theme song in true Ethel Merman fashion.

Something in the air at Pukaskwa, or perhaps in the water, stirs the human impulse to create. I put on my rain gear one afternoon and clambered up a ridge that ringed the little cove where we were sheltered. I was delighted to find that some of the blueberries had ripened. I was equally pleased and more than a little surprised to come across a tiny *inuksuk* some previous hiker had erected on one promontory. Nearby was a rock that looked for all the world like a miniature version of a stone head from Easter Island. In several other spots along the shore, we came upon stacked rocks, particularly interesting pieces of driftwood, or stones honed and polished by the elements into playful shapes. These had been deliberately set aside as if to say to other passersby: "Hey, check this out. This is really cool." I am not dismayed to see these things, for they have none of the in-your-face temerity of graffiti. They are, rather, evidence that someone gave rein to his or her child's heart and sense of wonder. What could be better than that?

The Pukaskwa pits may have had a more deliberate purpose than that of creative self-expression. Nobody knows for certain what that purpose was. I, for one, am fully satisfied to simply let the mystery be. The pits are shallow indentations found on the raised stone beaches of what was the shoreline of Lake Superior centuries ago. The indentations are each rimmed with stones in an oblong or circular pattern. Perhaps they are gravesites. Perhaps they served as meat caches. Perhaps they had a spiritual function for an animist people long since forgotten. On Otter Island, several of these pits are situated well in from the shore in what seems to be an array surrounded by a low stone wall. We all speculated on the reason for the existence of these structures, coming no closer to solving their mystery. One gains a strong sense here that this is indeed sacred ground.

In following Paul's fine example, I hope to become a far more observant hiker. The Pukaskwa Coastal Hiking Trail parallels the shore from Hattie Cove to a spot near Newman Bay, a distance of about thirty-seven miles. Paul led James and me on a walk along part of this trail one evening. He wanted us to check out what he thought was a bear's den that he had previously spotted. He quietly pointed out several mosses, lichens, and Indian pipe saprophytes along the way. There was nothing at all disingenuous in his interest for what he was experiencing, and the intensity of his focus was simply contagious. He walked calmly with his hands clasped behind his back as if out for a pastoral stroll. Paul shared that walking in Pukaskwa Park felt to him as if he were walking through a temperate rain forest. It was certainly green, damp, and virile enough to have been somewhere in the Pacific Northwest. There was the possibility that what he found was indeed used as a hibernating or birthing den for bears. A bruin could have far worse digs. No, I did not give in to his suggestion that I crawl down to check for current inhabitants.

James is kindhearted and particularly generous in sharing his skills. The waves out on the big lake kept us penned in a sheltered bay one afternoon. Sally was keen to add to her repertoire of kayaker self-rescue techniques. There are several ways a paddler can re-enter an overturned kayak, and James used both my kayak and his own to help Sally practice a few of these. His patience and encouragement was an excellent match for Sally's spirit and drive. Sally would be hard pressed to fall out of a boat as large as the Harris family tandem. However, if she ever wants to do a cannonball off its deck, she will be able to get back in the boat.

Of course, when one has a plethora of camping equipment, a certain amount of time and effort must be given up to maintenance. When I think of Paul Harris, one image will always come to mind. We were situated at our pullout site at Hattie Cove waiting for the shuttle van to bring us all back to Michipicoten Harbor. Gear was strewn all over the place in various piles. Tents and clothing were draped across shrubs and tree branches in hopes that a little drying might occur before everything got packed for the long ride home. Paul was deeply into a role as Mr. Meticulous. He was searching for something to take the gummy residue of duct tape off the front deck of his beautiful kayak. First he tried a good deal of elbow grease. Then he tried white wine as a solvent in addition to his elbow grease and found this to be surprisingly effective. He finally took a bit of white gas from the camp stove fuel tank to finish the job. I had to admire the fellow's innovative persistence. I hope he will forever be able to distinguish white gas from white wine. Both are useful liquids, but they are not entirely interchangeable.

It is the company you keep that makes the greatest difference in who you are and who you will one day become. Though I have come to fully appreciate the restorative power of wilderness solitude, I also realize how richly blessed I have been to encounter such a wealth of fellow paddlers. Pukaskwa is far too large and too wild a place to keep to one's self. The joy stirred inside me was put there to share.

Finding Balance

A S WITH ANY watercraft, maintaining proper balance in a kayak is essential to its safe and efficient forward momentum. Finding your center of gravity, knowing your limits and to what extent they can be pushed, understanding what does and does not constitute a reasonable risk; all of these elements swim through your consciousness to keep you from swimming in the drink. When people learn that I take a kayak trip on Lake Superior each summer, they often ask, "Do you roll?" The trick is not to have to roll, and this is especially true when the better part of a week's worth of food and gear is in your hatches weighing you down and needing to remain dry. A touring kayak is actually more stable with a load. Of course, that is only true as long as the paddler is adept at finding balance.

I return to the Canadian shore of Lake Superior repeatedly because it is there that I am assured of finding peace. In order to maintain proper balance in my life, I need to go wilding on occasion. Wilding does not constitute rampage in my lexicon. It simply means that I reverently reconnect with my maker in a natural setting and unplug all that is extraneous. Returning to an unspoiled, wild shore that never fails to bring joy allows me to reflect, to go deep, and to peel back the rind on a place or a problem in order to have a good look inside.

When I returned to Lake Superior's Pukaskwa Coast in July of 2009, there were several issues stemming from my job as a special education teacher that had me seriously out of kilter. I was nearing my thirty-year mark working with a suburban Minneapolis school district teaching reading and English to deaf and hard-of-hearing students. The job I had once loved was no longer fresh or satisfying. Most days had me feeling stymied, as if I were forever treading water. At that time, many instructional service providers working to better the lives of children with disabilities in the public sector were caught in a hopeless quagmire of state and federal regulations. Every major regulation came with its own mudslide of paperwork. Time spent on paperwork and in meetings meant less time available for directly interacting with needy students. My caseload burgeoned untenably to fifty-two clients, ranging from kindergarteners to adults in vocational training. Most students enrolled in special education programs ended up with a ream or two of required documentation by the time they graduated. Had I hired on to be a legal secretary? I had always dreamed of becoming a writer, but this was not at all what I intended. Repeatedly, I simply stuffed the frustration to get on with the task at hand. I was hoping all the while that what seethed inside me would not boil over irreparably.

A person is able to sustain such a self-destructive strategy for only so long. Well before the end of the school year, I was sorely in need of time on the water; time to heal, time to reflect, time to plan, and time to regain some semblance of balance. When summer finally arrived, Maggie and I rented a quiet cabin on Madeline Island just off the Wisconsin shore of Lake Superior. One of the first events of our week on the island was my getting bit in the butt by a loose dog while Maggie and I were out for a walk. It seemed so emblematic of my school year and the way I was feeling about my career. The dog was not rabid. It was a hard bite, but what pained me more was the owner's refusal to apologize or acknowledge any responsibility for control over the animal.

Maggie is and has always been an exceptionally kind and supportive spouse. She began her own teaching career before I did and recognized my symptoms. We spent a lot of time talking, strolling on the island's beaches, and doing our best to keep each other happy. We targeted the parts of our life together that brought us the greatest joy, and we did our best to keep at bay anything that created anxiety. With Maggie's help, I would in time create a scheme for pulling away from teaching and moving ahead to whatever came next. That was not yet on the horizon. We returned home for a short while. Then, with more need than I knew how to express, I went off wilding once again up to the Canadian shore of Lake Superior to paddle and to garner peace.

Three days into my paddle trip from Hattie Cove to Michipicoten Harbor, my three kayaking companions and I were finding an abundance of bliss exploring

Ontario's Pukaskwa National Park. We were paddling the waters of the largest freshwater lake on the planet, but it could be the size of a wading pool for all we could see. Fog made it necessary to stay together and to stay near the shore. Our foursome was heading to Cascade Falls, a magical place of wild and pristine beauty. The other three paddlers had never seen this place before, and I was becoming concerned that the fog would diminish their experience. I had paddled in this area twice previously, and I love how this falls dumps straight into Lake Superior without any fuss—it is just a simple curve and a downward plunge. Most of the waterfalls pouring into this lake have a configuration like the knuckles of a hand, with several chutes more or less together. There is typically a sandbar at the juncture of river and lake. Such is not the case with Cascade.

I need not have worried. The fog actually enhanced the beauty of this sacred place, giving it a tinge of the surreal. Judging from the smiles on my three companions, Cascade Falls struck a responding chord in each of us. The thundering pulse of this torrent drowned out all the other noises that cluttered my mind. I found that exceedingly therapeutic. A pummeling shower in the falls just about had me losing my shorts. We had a leisurely lunch, and as we stretched to relax, the sky cleared. That is one thing I have learned about worry: If you simply let it go and refuse to allow it to sap your energies, you often find the fog has lifted.

The weather turned against us the following morning, and we became windbound for most of the day at a cobble beach on Richardson Island. We spent much of our drizzly captivity reading, chatting, and baking in the shelter of a tarp while waiting for the wind and waves to lessen. We were eager to round the headland of Pointe La Canadienne and enter the sheltered waters of Imogene Cove. There is a long, beautiful stretch of beach there, and it is a fine place to camp.

By late afternoon, we were trying to balance our impatience with a reasonable assessment of our mutual skill set in order to gain an honest measure of the danger facing us. We decided to make a tricky surf launch and go for it. Even with a wet suit, a rain jacket, and a high-waisted neoprene spray skirt, wave splashes sent cold water right into my core. I tried to remember to loosen the grip on my paddle so as not to risk the same tendonitis that plagued me when I first got into this sport. We were all in for one wild ride.

This was a calculated risk. There are many such choices made each day on a paddle trip. However, if you really stop and think about it, this was no more dangerous than hurling down the expressway amid a sea of motorists, any of whom could turn you into a bug splat with one false move. The wind, the swells, and the reverberation waves made for a long and stressful stint of paddling. The conditions were worst near the shoals and just off the headland. We tried our best to stick close together. I had never paddled in stuff this rough. Flashes popped into my consciousness from my third-grade catechism class. Specifically, I recalled a proclamation attributed to Saint Augustine:

"He who sings prays twice." A blend of my fear, adrenaline, and exhilaration gave voice to invocation. What started out as a thought inside of me quickly became a voiced prayer. This prayer became a shout when the waves sent their worst my way. It morphed into a song when both the waves and I gentled a bit. Finally, it became a hymn of thanksgiving. If a fellow sings, prays, and paddles all in the same set of motions, is he in fact executing a spiritual trifecta?

A knot of tension the size of a fist lodged right between my shoulder blades. It became even more pronounced as we made the final turn around the point. Here the combination of wind gusts, currents, and reverberation waves all made the waters very confused. Control seemed difficult to attain. I could, however, maintain both balance and forward momentum. This was enough to get the job done. The four of us each dealt with the struggle separately but successfully, and we hit the beach at Imogene Cove relieved and exhausted. With a fine supper, a mug of wine, and the joyful camaraderie of kindred souls around a campfire, that knot of tension between my shoulder blades evaporated entirely.

Imogene Cove is an excellent place for a layover day. The moldering remnants of an extensive logging operation and the tiny community that rose around it are scattered all about and slowly sinking into the moss. The loggers pulled out for good in 1930. In time, this forest will heal itself entirely and cover up all scars. As I joined my tripmates to explore the area, I became fully immersed in the immediate. I was buoyant, and whatever stowaway worries accompanied me to the Pukaskwa Coast were for the moment as gone as yesterday's wind and waves.

If turning off that part of the mind that fuels anxiety were as simple as flipping a switch, perhaps my spirit would have no need for wilderness. People, though, are not made that way. One of my fellow kayakers teased me at sundown as I knelt on the cobbles scrubbing the dinner dishes, a task I thoroughly enjoy. She told me that I had most definitely slipped into my nothing box. This, supposedly, is the place where the males of our species need to go from time to time in order to get away from having to think. There could be something to this. Have I the power to turn off mental tension simply by engaging in mindless activity? Surely, that is worth risking a case of dishpan hands.

We left our Imogene Cove enclave and took full advantage of the excellent paddling conditions. We polished off most of our miles each day during the morning hours before the wind and waves started kicking. This permitted time to explore inland a bit each afternoon, which all of us were well inclined to do. Our campsite at Ghost River was in an area just east of the Pukaskwa Coast. This piece of shoreline is known as The Flats, but only because it is low relative to the nearby headlands. It is rugged enough. Seeking some time alone, I headed inland and upstream with my fly rod to explore the river. I figured if I could make my way to a small lake shown on the map, the fish just might be in a mood to cooperate.

It did not take long for reality to sink in and for me to accept that this was not the river to fish. This was the river to explore. I made my way over and around several deadfalls and then began to climb. Ghost River is shallow and clear near its mouth. There were no signs of fish. I kept climbing, knowing exactly what I was after but finding something entirely different. Where was there a substantial falls with a deep plunge pool full of brook trout? Maybe if I climbed farther, I decided. This first cataract was spectacular, though, even with its shallow pool. The rocks along the river were like a staircase. Having nine feet of fly rod in my hand forced me to go slow and to step carefully. One poorly placed foot on a slippery rock would have totally trashed this old fellow. I climbed up four such cataract staircases before turning back, and each was higher and even more spectacular than the last. No fish, but there were gnarled cedar roots, blue flag irises, and tiny silver and white rivulets splashing down through cracks in black rock. It was a marvelous Lilliputian universe I would never have discovered were it not for my desire to catch and release wild trout.

I returned to the campsite without having made a single cast and without having seen the small lake that was my objective. Still, the joy inside of me could not have been richer had I caught a boatload of trout. Sometimes it is enough to set out without rigid adherence to any objective and to simply allow some room in your life for surprise and delight.

There is usually some sort of song coming from my kayak when I am happy. Indeed, my singing, as out of tune as it may be, is an accurate barometer for my mood. I was successful in shelving the tensions that had accompanied me to this wild coast, at least for the time being. It was as though some unsuspecting soul had just fed my inner coin slot with about a ton of quarters and flipped the switch on my wilderness Wurlitzer. I know the words to dozens of songs, and they showed up en masse at the threshold of my consciousness when all that bleak anxiety had left by the back door. They may or may not have been the correct words. My recalling the correct melody seemed of less consequence than simply being vocal. Remember what I said about forward momentum? Usually, I am out of earshot of others when I let loose musically. My true purpose in the woods may be nothing more than to provide entertainment for the chipmunks. Music is made visible in the coursing of waves and in the way the wind tosses the pine tops. As long as I can go wilding now and then to maintain balance, and as long as I can see this wild music, what do I have to fear from deafness?

When our group of paddlers entered the mouth of the Dog River, I headed for the backside of the giant sandbar and pulled my kayak well up on shore, out of the grip of the current. Anticipation was on the rise inside of me. When you spend three years dreaming of your return to a place you love and then actually make your return, can that place rise to meet your expectations? When that spot is Denison Falls of the Dog River and your dream is all about fly-fishing for rainbow trout, the answer is a resounding *yes!* I first came here in the summer of 2006, and had less than two hours to fish before our group needed to make the long hike back to the campsite at the mouth of the river. On this return trip, I was blessed with a great abundance of time and was able to fish to my heart's content. It took time, too, in order to figure out just how deep the trout were and just what would entice them to respond. They were quite deep, and I had to crimp tin shot onto my tippet and use the heaviest nymphs in my box. The payoff was phenomenal. I released all but one fine rainbow, and this we had for supper. A friend once taught me how to poach trout in wet cedar fronds over a wood fire, and I put this method to good use. The cooking took only about ten minutes, and the results were excellent.

Combining fly-fishing with kayak tripping on Lake Superior works amazingly well as a tension eraser. The final campsite of our paddle trip was near the mouth of Dore River. This fine spot, with its giant whaleback rock, seems surprisingly wild considering how near it is to civilization. If you cock your head a bit when out on the rocks here, you can see some of the buildings of the nearby First Nation settlement. I did not spend much time fishing below the falls, though I am told this can be a particularly good spot for large trout. My fishing gear was light tackle, and what I sought once again was a grand balance of fly angling and exploration. I headed up to the pond above the falls and skirted the left shoreline until I reached the first little swift. Casting into the bubble line at the end of this swift met with the anticipated result. The place was brimming with scrappy, hungry little brook trout. I was in heaven.

Balance is an odd and often elusive thing. I have shared that balance is what I sought from the start of this set of experiences. That is because at the time of my trip, I did not have all the correct words with which to frame what was so painfully unsettled inside of me. Paddling down the Pukaskwa Coast and beyond as I did may seem nothing more than pure escapism. It may seem that I was riding toward an inevitable fall. However, in this wild setting, clarity and definition both began to seep into my consciousness. Having successfully gone wilding once more, I was more confident in my ability to take care of myself without all that useless wallowing in self-doubt. Some of that confidence I would put to good use in my trying to deal with the challenges of my city self. Once again, I had experienced daily reminders of just how happy I was capable of being and how easily I am able to contribute to the joy of those around me. There has long been this awful dichotomy. What I do for a living conflicts mightily with what I do for a life. Something would have to yield. Though a bit blue with the close of this journey, I was already kindling a strong spark of hope. I felt a deep sense of thanksgiving for blessings freely given and gratefully received.

Each evening when I pitch my tent, I have a ritual. The final thing I do before calling the task finished is to inflate a silly blow-up gnome named Little Hughie. Hughie stands guard outside my tent to keep the bears away. He serves to remind me not to ignore the little boy inside of me. He also helps me remember to take it easy on the river rock hops, for my beard is every bit as white as his. I am not the young man I once was. Looking at Hughie reminds me not to take myself so darn seriously. There are days when we are both full of hot air. Without proper balance, both Hughie and I would topple.

It brings me great joy to know that the little boy inside of me is still very much alive and is still full of a sense of wonder. It is this side of me that wanted to turn my boat around at Perkwakwia Point and head back along the coast up to Pukaskwa once again. I was choked up to where I found it difficult to speak as Rock Island came into view, signaling the end of our journey. The water was particularly kind this final morning, as was the sky. The lake became a mirror. Mist was rising. The still-distant cloudbank and its fog held off until we rounded Rock Island and went ashore.

Check the Flip Side

Picture the Lake Superior water trail from the international border at Pigeon River to the tiny village of Rossport, Ontario, as one long beaded necklace. The myriad islands to the west and east of Sibley Peninsula are the beads, and the star gem is the peninsula itself. On the southern tip of Sibley Peninsula is a set of spectacular mesas that give the appearance of an outsized kayaker who just stepped out of his boat and set down his paddle to take a nap with his arms folded across his chest. Of course, your interpretation may take on a different style depending on your preferences. This is Naniboujou, the sleeping giant, who figures richly in the culture and traditions of the Anishinaabe people. Climb on up and your efforts will be rewarded with a view of Lake Superior you are likely to find humbling. It would be difficult to gaze out from here and not be in awe of the vastness of these waters. Do watch your step. Fall from here and you are not going to be getting up in a hurry.

You can certainly paddle this route in less than the two weeks I took, but why rush a good thing? The beauty of kayaking through an extended archipelago is that it offers you so many paddling options. You can often dodge the worst of the wind and waves by tucking in behind an island or two. Take a breather at the leeward or flip side of an island before you continue working your semi-sheltered way from point to point. When the wind finally does shut you down, you can usually find a suitable shelter to set up camp. The variety here is appealing, also. You could paddle among these islands for years and never do exactly the same route twice. Thankfully, much of this area is now protected from future development, having recently been set aside as part of the Lake Superior National Marine Conservation Area.

When the winds do drive you ashore, it is time for hiking, beachcombing, berry picking, cooking, or catching the express train to Snoozeville to go a few rounds with Mr. Sandman. Take your cue from Naniboujou. He has been in a state of repose here for a good long while. The latent nest builder in me loves establishing a new home every evening in an entirely different waterfront setting. It comes without property taxes. No one will ever try to foreclose on my tent. I have done this kind of paddling for several years now, and each year I try to pare my gear down even more. That being said, it is funny how some items once seen as extravagant are now necessary concessions to old age and sore muscles. Camping here without a good, thick sleeping pad would be inconceivable now, but I used to scoff at such luxuries. The number of medications in my Dopp kit gets a bit larger every summer. Still, I would be a liar if I said kayaking on Lake Superior the way I do did not make me feel years younger every trip.

Kayaks are not the only crafts coursing through these waters. This is a pleasure boater's paradise. The abundance of yachts and motorboats, each tricked out with multiple downriggers, gives testimony to this region of Lake Superior being a prime sport fishery. These fisher folk seek lake trout and Chinook salmon. I favor brook trout on a light fly rod. However, save for the odd coaster brookie working the shallows for bugs, my route among these northern islands is not all that conducive to the kind of fishing I most dearly love.

In truth, I came here fishing for a healing calm. Thankfully, there is no scarcity of peace among these islands. People I deeply care about have been recently plagued by dissolution, as marriages chill and life partners seek to redefine themselves. I can truthfully, humbly, and most gratefully say that my own marriage is stronger now than it has ever been. The same is true of my faith. Disillusion has also plagued more than one dear friend of mine, and this has come with career-shattering consequences. I have not been entirely spared from this. The 2009-2010 school year was to be my last as a teacher. Immediately prior to the start of this kayak trip, I took a leap of faith. I stepped away from my career as a special education instructor, choosing after three decades to steer my life into a different channel, not at all certain where it might lead. I was hungry for a change.

Of course, I will miss the kids. How could I not miss the kids and remain human? Some of the images of a career spent working with children are indelibly etched in my soul. Being witness to a hard-of-hearing child's first experience with amplification and the saucer-eyed look of wonder that initial fitting creates is an unforgettable miracle. I can readily conjure the memory of a favorite kindergartner Maggie and I worked with years ago. He referred to his auditory trainer unit as his radio and wore it with great pride. One of his classmates asked me if he got to listen to Raffi all day instead of to the teacher. I have found the spontaneous hug from a first-grader quite healing. The jack-o-lantern grin and high five of a young man with Down's syndrome can be a perfect antidote to weeks of dealing with middle-schoolers' surly attitudes. No, I will not miss drowning in paperwork.

So, I took to the wild coast of Superior once again. As is my wont, I began the transition to this new life chapter with a paddle trip. There are certainly many other waters I could explore. However, in deference to the contemplative side of my being, I prefer to concentrate my travel and add depth to each trip. I seek to experience all that I can from a single spectacular area rather than proceed broadly in a hopscotch manner and experience only what appears on the surface. It is my desire to get to know the north coast of Lake Superior intimately and to bank on a sure bet. Time and again, I will gratefully return to where I am certain to find peace in abundance, bringing to these waters my hungry senses.

Keep your senses open and your ego in a box and you have quite a lot to learn from the people with whom you travel. I have been greatly blessed that way over the years, as a mutual passion for paddling these waters has connected me with some amazing individuals. You might think an academic who has spent much of his career underground studying bats and the biology of caves would be about as exciting as day-old toast. Not so. My professorial paddling companion was a totally engaging fellow who loosened up considerably once he was out on the water. His curiosity was infectious. Together we explored many of the niches, nooks, and fissures of the islands we passed, and we poked the bows of our kayaks into whatever looked interesting. He helped me to experience so much more from this environment than I would ever see on my own, and I am greatly indebted to him because of this.

There are certain key images and memories that cannot help but rush to your consciousness in a flood when you reflect upon a special place or event. When I consider these islands, I can easily conjure up the hike to an overlook on Spar Island called Top of the World. It could easily have been redubbed Bottom of the Well the day we visited, socked in as we were by fog. Limited views notwithstanding, the hike was a terrific leg stretcher. I took my cues from my academic companion and from the weather conditions. The fog shroud caused us to focus more intently on the micro paradise at our feet comprised of tiny mushrooms, club mosses, and lichens. Were they there all along?

What you see on the surface is rarely all there is. This is as true of the wilderness here as it is of the people passing through it. Gazing at the lakeward side of Pie Island, you would be hard-pressed to find a wilder shore on Lake Superior. However, within sight from the landward flip side of this same island is the city of Thunder Bay, Ontario, a vibrant metropolis with a population topping 108,000 souls. So, too, this lake has just as many moods as I have. Take for granted these halcyon days and she will send a storm your way to slap you back into reality.

A kayaker cannot go from Pie Island to the western tip of Sibley Peninsula without crossing an exceptionally busy shipping channel. This is the entrance to the Port of Thunder Bay. The passage is about ten kilometers, and I watched the boat traffic from the comfort and safety of our island campsite feeling much the way a stray dog must feel prior to crossing eight lanes of the Interstate. One does not play chicken with a freighter. Would our kayaks even form blips on ship radar? If so, would we be considered anything more significant than a few floating speed bumps?

It is best to give the big boys the right of way. There is no way they would be stopping for the likes of us.

Our trio was blessed with calm waters for the entire crossing. I speak only of my own emotions when I claim the passage began with a state of high anxiety. I was frantically keyed up and extremely vigilant lest we all become flattened flotsam. Halfway across, however, I became certain that each of us was experiencing fully the same blissful serenity. It was as though the peace of these tranquil waters had washed its way into the spirit core of us all. We paddled in silence the entire ten kilometers. There was no boat traffic save for ourselves, and only the shorebirds off Thunder Cape were witness to our passing.

Our portion of Lake Superior remained calm until mid-morning. The wind rose quickly, and white caps appeared by the time we paddled into Sibley Peninsula's Tee Harbor and set up camp. To call the deer around Tee Harbor tame is not entirely accurate, but it comes close. One large buck with a noble set of velvet-covered antlers must have taken it personally that we would have the effrontery to pitch our tents so close to his favorite patch of grass. He made plenty of noise stomping around in the wee hours, and he woke me. Actually, I owe him a debt of gratitude. His stirrings got me up and out of my tent. I was witness to more stars than I could ever hope to count in a perfectly clear night sky.

Most thieves are cowards and opportunists. This is every bit as true of red squirrels, chipmunks, and whiskey jacks as it is of human beings. One persistent and particularly greedy little chipper had haunches like a dually pickup truck. It seemed especially fond of pancakes, and I half expected it to grab a plate and ask me to pass the maple syrup. This overstuffed little scrounger had it made compared with its shy, scrawny cousin, who lingered at the edge of our lunch site. We had hiked up to the top of Naniboujou, the somnolent big fellow of Sibley Peninsula. If old Naniboujou had an appendectomy scar, it would be right about where we sat. Handouts for chipmunks up top in this paradise must be a bit scarce. This poor creature looked almost anorexic. I made a point of being extra clumsy with the gorp bag, spilling a little bit in hopes that it would be found after we departed.

From our high-country vantage point, we studied the effect sunshine and passing clouds had on the forest below. Light and shadow were in constant play with the trees, giving life, spirit, and magic to the scene. Likewise, the artistry in the interactions of light and shadow on the lake was mesmerizing. Watch these waters long enough and you will witness just about every hue of blue and green in the spectrum.

If you are well acquainted with the Canadian shore of Lake Superior, chances are good that you are familiar with the Group of Seven. Early in the last century, these artists helped to immortalize the Algonquian Wilderness, the Algoma Highlands, Georgian Bay of Lake Huron, and the Canadian shore of Lake Superior in their paintings. When I am snowbound, restless, and months away from being able to switch my inner clock to island time with a paddle trip, their fine artwork feeds my hungry soul and sustains me. It is always superb food for dreams. Many of the images they captured on canvas flashed through my mind as I engaged with the changing artistry of the views from atop Naniboujou.

Plump or puny chipmunks, hectic or halcyon days, calm or calamitous waters; there is an intriguing duality to things out here that a seeming lack of the in between accentuates. This duality reminded me of one of my favorite paintings, the subject of which is an island not all that distant from where we were paddling. The painting is *Pic Island, Lake Superior* by Lawren Harris, a principal member of Canada's Group of Seven. The sensuous curves of the island, as depicted by the artist, evoke a tranquility that is Lake Superior at her soothing best. The image Harris captured is his interpretation of the view of Pic Island from the mainland, looking out across Thompson Channel. I wonder if the artist ever had an opportunity to check out the flip side of his beloved island.

I had a chance to kayak out and around Pic Island a few years ago. Having done so, I now find the Lawren Harris painting all the more beguiling. If the shoreward side of this fine island is all voluptuous curves, the lakeward side is all angles. It reminds me of the duality of my own nature. On the lakeward side of the island are sheer cliffs from which giant boulders have toppled. There is an intriguing natural stone arch near the entrance to South Bay. The ledge rock shore of South Bay is all cracks and crevices. It is no place you would want to be in a storm. When Lake Superior is at her tumultuous worst, she takes out her fury by pounding this backside of Pic Island.

After a string of placid paddle days, our tiny group was forced to take shelter on one of the Saint Joseph Islands west of Rossport. We were pinned down by a fierce wind and large waves at a stunning campsite with a bit of a split personality. The cliffs on nearby Saint Ignace Island gave a significant amount of protection to the northwestern side of our campsite. We watched with hope, scanning the sky for even the smallest patch of blue as clouds came barreling over the cliffs all afternoon. The lakeward side was sheer madness. With all the shoals, the currents, and the driving wind, roller waves were hammering the shore from three directions. The sky began breaking up as evening progressed. Slants of light from the setting sun continually formed rainbow bits out over the seething lake. I thought of the Group of Seven once again, for suddenly there it was, the quintessential Lawren Harris sky.

The rocky point on the western side of Harry Island was our final campsite of this paddle trip. Before settling in and making our home for the night, we took a side trip out to Battle Island, with its stately lighthouse. The toss and bounce caused by a strong wind out of the east gave us a good workout and made for slow going. When I was directly below the promontory, I gazed up at the lighthouse windows. I recalled the details I had recently read of a gale in 1977 that sent horrific waves with ice chunks crashing into the lighthouse, breaking those windows. That seemed unbelievable. Those panes were more than seventy feet above the lake surface. Then I noticed just how far my kayak had drifted in the few minutes I had been gazing upward and struggling with vertigo. Make no mistake—there is a wicked power to be reckoned with once this lake starts kicking.

We moved eastward to Battle Island's lee side and hauled out for lunch. Not a soul was around at the lighthouse. Everything was locked. The light has long been automated, but a former keeper spends a portion of each summer on the site. The grounds were well maintained with obvious care. We had been hoping for a bit of a tour, but this was not to be. A quiet hour out of the wind was our consolation, and we welcomed that gratefully.

By the time we were all situated around a driftwood fire at our campsite on Harry Island, the wind had slackened considerably. It was a time for reflection. There was much ruminating shared. There was also much kept private. My key objective for this particular paddle trip had been to concentrate on the immediate. I promised myself that I would not grieve over that which I had recently left. I would not fear the future with all of its uncertainty. As I gazed into the fire, I knew that scheme had worked far better than I could have hoped. This trip was a uniquely satisfying set of experiences in the wild. It would be for me a wellspring of just the type of optimism I needed to launch into the next chapter in my life. There were three key requirements in my strategy for moving forward from my career as a teacher. These I had dutifully recorded in my trip journal. First, I would write. Second, I would be of service to humankind, doing something that made a positive difference in the lives of others. Third, I would continue to assist Maggie in the fulfillment of our mutual commitment to happiness.

Pushing ahead toward a simpler life would permit me the freedom to check out the flip side of my being.

Who would I discover once much of the old angst had evaporated? There would be abundant time to concentrate on a few long-deferred dreams. I had applied for a three-year leave of absence. This was granted. As long as I paid into my pension each of those three years, I could retire with full benefits once the leave had ended. That seemed a pretty fine deal. I stirred the coals with a stick and chuckled. As I spent each of the past fourteen days paddling from island to island, my heart had grown lighter. No doubt about it; this smile on my mug was bound to become more of a permanent fixture.

Of Kayaks and Concessions

So, WHY ARE you paddling with a guide? Do you still have training wheels on your kayak?" This came from my brother, and it was a fair question. Concessions made to keep you in the game may appear to rob you of independence. Perhaps you, too, once moved with the mantra *Go swift, quiet, and alone.* Along comes a shift in priorities or circumstances. It may not be of your own choosing, but there is a transformation that says *Swallow your pride and go with a guide.* You compromise in order to stay connected with your passion. I have discovered that such a shift need not be a bad thing.

A clumsy fight with gravity in 2012 kept me out of my kayak and off the big water for what seemed an eternity. Gravity had won. I slipped while trying to move down off a platform onto a rolling ladder. In an attempt to avoid landing on my noggin, I twisted and managed to slam my lower back hard against a step. Upon impact, a whole new constellation flashed before my eyes. X-rays found nothing broken. I was in a world of hurt, but there was every reason to believe the condition was merely temporary. If I had to go and bust myself up with a klutzy move, it was far better to have that happen ten minutes from the doctor's office than out on a paddle trip.

Most folks would find me far more the poster child for cussed stubbornness than anyone's role model of stalwart perseverance. I threw myself into a regimen of stretches, ibuprofen, massage, and physical therapy sessions. My focus was getting healthy in order to return to paddling as quickly as possible. However, nothing was making much of a positive difference. I still ached and was beginning to feel like a decrepit old man.

Perhaps life would have been easier had I changed my mantra to *Grow gray with grace*. I simply was not there yet. Ignoring the pain and trying to function just as before was not a wise course of action. I moved too fast too soon.

Figuring a day trip was certainly feasible, I tried to portage into a favorite trout lake with my kayak riding on my shoulder, threatening dislocation. I slipped and landed flat on my back in a pile of rocks. Pain and anger registered first. Then came a terrible sadness. My will was beginning to change. Maybe this way of connecting with the wilderness I so dearly loved was no longer possible. This lake is entirely within the Boundary Waters Canoe Area Wilderness, where kayak carts are not permitted. I turned to leave the trout alone and headed back to the landing utterly dejected.

There is a roof dent in my Subaru that continues to remind me of that aborted day trip and of my infernal impatience. It was a consequence of my stubborn refusal to yield to what was so painfully obvious. I had indeed reached the point where it is best to seek assistance whenever I try car topping my kayak. My internal dialogue from that struggle reflects a losing battle: *Well, rollers might do the trick. Maybe that nifty hoist system I saw on the Internet. The fool thing costs more than I paid for my first car. Sure, I am short enough and gray enough to garner sympathy at boat landings. There is usually some kind soul who is willing to help. But, damn, it is so embarrassing having to ask.*

So, what exactly is lethal about embarrassment? What did I have to prove to anyone by being stubbornly independent? A younger version of myself would have been happy to help anyone with a canoe or a kayak. All a person ever had to do was have the grace to ask. Swallow your pride. Give another the opportunity for a kindness that benefits both of you. I changed the track of my internal dialogue and paid attention.

My next visit to the doctor's office began with a lecture and ended with an MRI.

The results of the imaging showed that I had severe spinal stenosis. It was present at birth. That just goes to show you are never too old to learn something new about yourself. Thankfully, the condition was surgically correctable. Healing would need time, and that meant an entire summer without a paddle trip. If that hiatus meant returning to the water healthier and happier, it was a concession I was willing to make.

I had made a previous concession never to kayak alone on Lake Superior. This was a vow intended to help ease the anxiety of my loving, non-kayaking wife.

It turned out to be one of the best decisions of my life as a paddler. So far, I have kept my promise and have taken several superb paddle trips along the Canadian coast of Lake Superior, always with a guide. What I lose in self-sufficiency is of far less significance than what I gain from interacting with individuals in a wilderness environment. Besides, I have found that whenever my sense of independence flares with insistence and my ego rears up to assert itself defiantly, there is always a bit of reality to slap it back into place.

Permit me to share a case in point. On a layover day a few summers back, I broke free from my guide and fellow paddlers and spent time alone fly-fishing a mile or so below Denison Falls on the Dog River. While the others hiked the long path from our Lake Superior campsite to the top of the falls, I rock-hopped from point to point happily, in quest of rainbow trout. One misplaced foot on a mossy slick sent me careening down the granite bank straight into the drink. Icy water shocked me right out of my bliss. I hauled out on a rock immensely grateful to find neither cranium nor fly rod had shattered. It dawned on me how narrowly I escaped becoming flotsam. The image of my guide and fellow paddlers searching for my driftwood corpse spooked me mightily. God was my only witness, and I figured that I must have given quite a show. As soon as my shaking stopped, I began to laugh. My laughter echoed through the canyon.

There were periods when I wrestled with my decision to stop going it alone. That concession was never more lamented than during each annual Far North Paddle Trip Symposium in the Twin Cities. Though I am not anyone's groupie, I always gravitated to presenters who were solo trippers. One of these was Herb Pohl. His stories of paddle sojourns to Ungava, to Richmond Gulf, to the heart of Nunavut stirred the hunger in me for a trip of the long and lonesome kind. His freedom made me restless. I admired his stubborn pluck and his self-reliance. Then one day I learned first-hand just what that freedom cost.

A government helicopter landed on our beach campsite east of Pukaskwa National Park one afternoon in July of 2006. Whenever that happens, you know it is not going to be the Prize Patrol arriving with your sweepstakes winnings. Senses prickled and the needle on the uh-oh meter plunged to the red zone. Those aboard were searching for Herb Pohl, age seventy-six, whose solo boat had been retrieved at the mouth of the Michipicoten River with no sign of its owner. Days later, the group of which I was a part pulled into Naturally Superior Adventure's kayak center at Rock Island Lodge. We learned that Mr. Pohl's body had been recovered not far from the lodge, sans life jacket.

It is not my place to judge how or why this man perished. Still, I do know this much—he most certainly did leave a grieving family. Amid the pickup trucks and trailers in the parking lot at Rock Island Lodge, one stretch limousine looked grossly out of place. A funeral director was meeting with a somber, well-dressed lady, helping her make necessary arrangements. At the kind request of Rock Island's manager, I gave up the room I had reserved so this lady could spend the night on site. I booked a room in the nearby town of Wawa.

I remember reflecting that night how painful it is to try to make a balance with your passions in one pan of the scale and your loved ones in the other. I cannot promise my loved ones that nothing hurtful will ever come to them or to me as a result of my kayak trips. The people I love are not bargaining chips. Still, I remain unwilling to separate myself from my passion to paddle. As a concession to an older, less resilient, less forgiving body, I have chosen to give up some of my independence. That choice enhances the margin of safety so that I may continue to paddle as long as my spirit is willing.

My first kayak trip after spinal surgery was a return to the Pukaskwa Coast. I was back in the saddle and feeling great. One of the other trip members was a yoga instructor, who volunteered to teach us how to remain flexible and to ease muscle tension. That was certainly an unexpected blessing. Not only did I have a wonderful paddle trip, I also became one with my inner Gumby. With a limber body and a playful spirit, life is indeed rich.

Embers

B ANK A FIRE well and it is easy to rekindle. The journals, letters, and annotated maps that fill my den make it easy to reignite a paddle trip experience. Most of my reflections recount tremendous joy derived from exercising a true passion for a wilderness life. However, if I am any kind of paddler at all, I am the well-rounded sort. There have been plenty of darker hours. Ember gazing can also conjure the joyless events, bringing them once more to the surface. Picking at the memory of an unsuccessful experience is like picking at a scab. It often leads to the same result.

Over the decades, I have had my share of aborted paddle trips, canoes hopelessly trashed in rapids, maps misread, and sunken kettle packs. You can abandon a wrapped canoe a whole lot easier than you can jettison the painful memory of having messed up big time. Before I reached my mid-twenties, I was directly responsible for the loss of two canoes in rapids I had no business trying to run. Only by the grace of God have my tripmates and I been spared serious injury. It can be excruciating having to pull out of an experience mid-trip after investing so much of yourself in planning, effort, and dreaming. Though it may not seem at all possible when the mishap is fresh, you will become better for having pushed through the hurt. I learned this the hard way in the summer of 1982.

Our foursome was down to one canoe on the South Seal River after two of my tripmates wrapped their craft irretrievably around a boulder in a tricky swift. We tried for hours to unpin the canoe with no success. Our dream of paddling to Hudson Bay together was dead. Thankfully, each of us was physically unscathed. Next came the harsh realization of what we needed to make happen in order to reach safety. Ahead of us was a long slog back upriver to connect with folks at the Sayisi Dene First Nation settlement on Tadoule Lake.

We took turns roping the canoe up rapids and walking the riverbank. Once we reached Tadoule Lake, we shuttled gear and each other from point to point. A bonehead play on my part got us off course and delayed our reaching the settlement. This was a combination of my misreading a map and being literally lost in a fog.

It took us four days to work our way to the help we needed.

Fortunately, things began turning toward our favor. The Sayisi Dene people welcomed us warmly and let us use an empty cabin. A work crew from Manitoba Hydro was at the settlement, and they graciously allowed us to ride out with them on a flight to the Lynn Lake airbase where we had left our vehicle. They charged nothing for this kindness. Taking this flight meant I had to sell my canoe at the settlement, but there were several fellows eager to buy. We were soon on our way home. The trip had taken a heavy emotional toll. We were stressed out and ready to be thoroughly shed of each other by the time we reached Minneapolis.

Three summers later, I passed through this same area, once again headed to Hudson Bay. Unlike my aborted paddle trip, this journey was a *Pays-d'en-Haut* expedition. John Edmundson was once again in the lead. On the right shore at the end of the rapids I had come to know all too well was the broken-off bow section of a green canoe. I went to shore and examined it. Time, current, and ice had ripped it from the rest of the hull and tossed it up on the cobbles. Encountering this ruin set a twinge of pain coursing through me, for I knew its history. I also knew that the events connected to it had ended a friendship.

One of my earliest interactions with John involved a lost kettle/equipment pack. This was years ago, when we both worked at a canoe camp in Minnesota that is now defunct. He had been guiding a youth group in the Boundary Waters Canoe Area Wilderness when a moment of panic gave rise to a most unfortunate response. One of the canoe teams in the group John was leading swamped in a rapids. The stern paddler, who was John's co-guide, reacted by frantically heaving all the packs out of the canoe. This included the kettle pack, which sank irretrievably to the bottom of the river.

I can only speculate what this poor fellow was thinking at the time. I am sure he replayed the scene in his mind quite often afterward, always kicking himself. A clear head would have quickly determined there was no real danger to people or equipment, even with the canoe swamped. After all, this fellow was able to stand in the current where he had dumped. If he absolutely had to start tossing packsacks, just a slight alteration in his trajectory would have led to a much brighter outcome.

As is the case today, there were plenty of other folks passing through the area willing and able to lend a hand. John and his crew got a message back to the canoe camp of their predicament and carried on with their trip. As the camp outfitter, it was my responsibility to assemble a replacement kettle pack. The camp cook and I took a day and paddled to a spot where John could collect the pack on his way east. The remainder of his group's wilderness experience passed cheerfully. A bit further into the summer, John's packsack hurling co-guide was laughing about the incident. Call it a growing pain. He had become a far more relaxed group leader, and the paddlers in his charge enjoyed him immensely.

Routine procedures followed without any departure help ensure group safety, but that is only if every group member follows them religiously. One of our canoes dumped in a rapids pouring out of Seal Hole Lake on the *Pays-d'en-Haut* Thlewiaza River trip of 1988. The kettle/equipment pack was the only pack that would not float, and was routinely secured to a thwart in the canoe before being covered with a canoe spray deck. Not this time, however. In their haste to run an exciting piece of whitewater, the pair responsible overlooked this small but vital task. When their canoe capsized, the pack sank like a Buick. Fortunately, we had food galore. Unfortunately, we now had no pots or pans and no first aid kit.

Just prior to our encountering the rapids, I had gone to shore to check out a small fly-in cabin on Seal Hole. It was unlocked, and I had taken a good look inside. While the rest of the crew helped our two soggy tripmates dry out and reassemble, John and I took a canoe back to that cabin. From its well-equipped kitchen, we took only a frying pan, a one-quart pot, a galvanized bucket, a spatula, and a large spoon. There were many other kitchen pieces left. We helped ourselves, but we would not put anyone flying in to use the cabin in jeopardy. These items certainly helped us out of a jam, as we had more than a week left in our trip. This manner of saving grace is one reason such bush cabins are traditionally left unlocked.

Thankfully, we all got through the rest of our journey with no need of first aid supplies. Cups and matches were in the lunch pack, so we were good with that. We still had our camping stove and fuel. John asked each of us to carve a spoon. I carved a pair of chopsticks, and they served quite well. Our mealtime arrangements looked rather odd and rudimentary, but they added a certain liveliness to our journey. It took a while for two of our crewmembers to stop beating themselves up about the lost pack. In the end, though, everyone took it in stride. It was just one more memorable part of a grand adventure.

If our dreams are what we rely upon to sustain us, what must we do to sustain our dreams? All I can offer is what works best for me, even if that appears didactic. A fuller engagement with wilderness is what I advocate. Quiet contemplation in a natural setting can be amazingly enlightening and cathartic. Learn to be still. Disengage yourself from all contrivances. Minimize your distractions in order to maximize your receptiveness. Learn to listen with all of your senses. Give thanks.

As I shared at the outset, I have become my own ditty bag, filled with paddle trip memories and keepsake moments. To a significant extent, I have also become my own ditch kit. When a voyage goes totally awry, a ditch kit or bail-out bag is that small parcel a mariner keeps handy containing the bare essentials for survival. Certain material items must be a part of this bundle. However, I am referring to the intangibles. A complete kit had better contain a good supply of faith, self-reliance, sound judgment, experience, and forgiveness. These are the essentials that sustain my dreams as well as myself. When preparing for a paddle trip, gratitude is the first thing this old paddler puts in his packsack. Gratitude is what I bring to each fireside.

Afterword

RECONNECTION IS WHAT I am after each time I paddle, and that is what keeps me on the water. Through the years, most of what sustains me in the wild has been simultaneously humbling and invigorating. I was raised to always share a good thing. Here, then, is a journal entry from my most recent Lake Superior kayak trip.

Someone dropped me in a giant vat of milk. I had to paddle my way to the rim. The refrigerator that is Lake Superior makes a great deal of thick fog on many of these July mornings when the warm air passing over the land collides with that sitting atop the perpetually cold water. The fog this morning was thoroughly engulfing. Navigation was often reduced to a game of inches. There is an additional anomaly along this northern coast. The amount of iron in much of the shore rock sometimes diddles with the compass needle. All of this can make travel exceedingly frustrating. It is best to concede from the get-go that the big lake is the one who is boss.

More often than not, I will welcome a foggy Lake Superior morning. Such conditions typically mean the winds are down and the seas are fair, at least for a little while. It took a while for me to master the lessons intrinsic to such a morning, but I would like to believe that I finally have it. I have abandoned any notion of my being in charge, for the reality of my circumstances kept hammering at me to sharpen my focus. How often must a person be slapped right out of the goal set for a day or for an entire experience before he or she stops being blinded by the obvious? It is best to park any preconceived agenda and savor what is given.

I love the way a thick fog forces a paddler to focus on the immediate. It fully captures your attention and keenly ratchets up each of your senses. I think we all need this from time to time. Refocus on what is given. Do not waste the day at hand pining for the day to come.

When I could not see more than a yard off the bow of my kayak, I looked down. The water could not have been any clearer, and there was enough light penetrating to make the lake bottom visible. I had the sensation of rapidly flying over an amazing world of striped and swirled boulders, no two entirely alike. In a place where I might easily have given up to the discouragement of a shroud of fog, I felt an amazing freedom. The fog became a comforter in a double sense of the word, and I was exceedingly happy.

Acknowledgements

I owe a debt of gratitude to several good souls who read early drafts of this book and provided helpful insight. Chief among these folks are Gay Lynne Liebertz and Elizabeth Jarrett Andrew. I am thankful to Ken Rusk for his perpetual enthusiasm and his unfailing encouragement. His deep love of wilderness greatly inspires those of us lucky enough to know him. My gratitude extends to the legion of paddle trippers over the decades with whom I have shared sun, rain, portage trails, and many a welcome campfire. A special nod goes to John Edmundson.

Without the kind oversight and cheerful advice of the staff at North Star Press, this book would never have shifted beyond the dreaming stage. Therefore, kudos go to Corinne Dwyer, Anne Rasset, and Curtis Weinrich. Much love and endless thanks go to Maggie for being such a wonderful wife and a friend beyond measure.

About the Author

Timothy McDonnell grew up in the wilderness of northeastern Minnesota on the periphery of the Boundary Waters Canoe Area Wilderness. He spent decades teaching English and reading skills to deaf and hard-of-hearing students in suburban Minneapolis. By avocation, he is an avid paddle tripper, writer, and dreamer. Since his retirement, Timothy spends his time writing and doing volunteer work for a Twin Cities non-profit organization that helps individuals transition out of homeless shelters and into independent living.

When Timothy is not in the woods, he is either writing about the woods or dreaming about his next paddle journey. This is his second book. North Star Press of Saint Cloud, Inc., published his first book, *The Whole Forest for a Backyard: A Gunflint Trail Wilderness Memoir*, in 2013. Ask for it at your favorite independent bookseller.